BEFRIENDING
ST JOSEPH

"I love this book. Through original prayers and meditations and perfectly wrought, imaginative narratives built on scripture and tradition, Deacon Greg Kandra helps us find this most silent of saints—a great listener of a saint, to be sure—by drawing us into those moments of his life about which we know: some profound, some nearly unfathomable, some that seem fairly ordinary until we really think about them. No one is better than Kandra when it comes to finding and sharing with us the small, nuanced points that are sometimes missed within the grand and ongoing pageant that is our salvation."

Elizabeth Scalia
Editor-at-large
Word on Fire Catholic Ministries

"One of the main reasons I admire St. Joseph is that he didn't let fear or inconvenience stop him from doing what God wanted him to do. While it's true that none of Joseph's words are recorded in the Bible, his actions tell us all we need to know. In *Befriending St. Joseph*, Deacon Greg Kandra leads us through the life of this great saint in a relevant and practical way. Reading this book has increased my desire to trust God's plan even when I don't fully understand all the details."

Gary Zimak
Author of *Give Up Worry for Lent!*

"Leave it to Greg Kandra—a devoted husband, deacon, and quintessential storyteller—to lead us closer to Jesus through meditations on the life of humble St. Joseph. Innovative and inspirational, *Befriending St. Joseph* breathes new life and insight into a traditional devotion as Kandra invites us to consider Joseph as the perfect companion for our daily challenges and everyday joys."

Lisa M. Hendey
Founder of CatholicMom.com

"Deacon Greg Kandra's *Befriending St. Joseph* is an absolute gift for me as a young father, a working professional, and a Catholic man striving to be holy. St. Joseph is far from the seemingly inaccessible images of Jesus's father-on-earth that I grew up with. Kandra paints a vivid and relatable picture of a father confronting the joys, doubts, insecurities, challenges, and triumphs of raising a child and serving as a husband. Don't let the brevity of this little book fool you; it's packed with prayerful insights that you'll return to over and over again."

Joel Stepanek
Vice president of parish services
Life Teen International

BEFRIENDING
ST JOSEPH

Finding Faith, Hope, and Courage
in the Seven Sorrows Devotion

DEACON GREG KANDRA

AVE MARIA PRESS AVE Notre Dame, Indiana

© 2022 by Greg Kandra

Founded in 1865, Ave Maria Press is a ministry of the United States Province of Holy Cross.

www.avemariapress.com

Paperback: ISBN-13 978-1-64680-137-4

E-book: ISBN-13 978-1-64680-138-1

Cover image, "The Most Chaste Heart of St. Joseph" © 2021 Natalia Zieba-Buscemi, www.benedictaboutique.com.

Cover and text design by Christopher D. Tobin.

Printed and bound in the United States of America.

Library of Congress Cataloging-in-Publication Data
Names: Kandra, Greg, author.
Title: Befriending St. Joseph : finding faith, hope, and courage in the
   seven sorrows devotion / Deacon Greg Kandra.
Description: Notre Dame, Indiana : Ave Maria Press, [2022] | Includes
   bibliographical references. | Summary: "Greg Kandra leads the reader on
   a journey of exploration and spiritual renewal rooted in biblical
   stories of Joseph and the centuries-old devotion known as the Seven
   Sorrows of St. Joseph"-- Provided by publisher.
Identifiers: LCCN 2021055838 (print) | LCCN 2021055839 (ebook) | ISBN
   9781646801374 (paperback) | ISBN 9781646801381 (ebook)
Subjects: LCSH: Joseph, Saint--Prayers and devotions.
Classification: LCC BX2164 .K36 2022 (print) | LCC BX2164 (ebook) | DDC
   242/.76--dc23/eng/20220111
LC record available at https://lccn.loc.gov/2021055838
LC ebook record available at https://lccn.loc.gov/2021055839

Dedicated with love and gratitude
to all the Josephs in my life, especially
George Joseph Kandra
Joseph Kandra
Msgr. Joseph A. Funaro
Rev. Francis Joseph Passenant
Ryan Joseph Keller
and the Sisters of St. Joseph,
Chestnut Hill, Pennsylvania

CONTENTS

INTRODUCTION

An old joke that you may now come across as a meme goes: "Here's my favorite quote from St. Joseph, '_____.'" This may be worth a small chuckle, but Joseph, spouse of Mary, earthly father of Jesus, "the silent Saint," enjoys a reputation that reaches back to the earliest days of Christianity and endures today. St. Joseph, as it turns out, has much to say to us and we have so very much to learn from him.

This book gives you a fresh take on a centuries-old devotion, the Seven Sorrows of St. Joseph, offering twenty-first–century Catholics a simple format with which to ponder Joseph's role in our salvation and the chance to learn from and pray with this towering patron of the Christian faithful.

Here, I have to offer a confession: I never quite realized how big an impact Joseph had on my own life and the influence he exerted over it until I began my formation as a deacon. My pastor, Msgr. Joseph Funaro, had a great love for St. Joseph and preached about him often. As many Italians like to do, Msgr. Funaro never missed an opportunity to celebrate the saint's feast day by inviting people to the rectory for the traditional delicacy, zeppole, a kind of scrumptious Italian doughnut.

Msgr. Funaro once reminded us in a homily that Joseph was not perfect—he was a sinner like the rest us, he explained—which was, to my simple brain, just mind-blowing. I suspect in the Catholic imagination (or, at least, in mine), this stoic figure is usually seen as only slightly less perfect than his spouse, Mary. But there is nothing in the Church's teaching (let alone in scripture) to indicate he was sinless. He had flaws. He may have had a temper. He faced temptations. One tradition holds that he was older when he wed Mary and so may have had another family and grown children, which raises the specter of another spouse, another story, before the one captured in scripture. We just don't know. All of which makes Joseph and his life mysterious, compelling, and yet really quite relatable.

Over time, I came to realize how many "Josephs" had been a part of my life (this book is dedicated to them) and how their quiet prayers to him, perhaps on my behalf, had brought me to where I am today. It almost seems inevitable that I would end up writing a book about him—one that, I hope, celebrates his humanity and sees him as a man in full.

The devotion we explore in this book, focused on the sorrows and joys of Joseph's life helps, I believe, to transform the plaster saint of side altars and night tables into a figure of flesh and blood—a man we all can relate to in one way or another.

THE DEVOTION

While the exact origins of this devotion are unclear, the tradition holds that it began with a shipwreck. In a nineteenth-century book, *The Annals of St. Joseph*, we find the story of two Franciscans who were traveling by ship along the coast of Belgium, when a storm hit and the ship sank. The two men stayed alive by clinging to some wreckage and praying to St. Joseph. At one point in the storm, the saint appeared to the men and helped them to safety. Joseph, it is reported, taught them to say seven Our Fathers and seven Hail Marys, and meditate on the seven passages in the Bible where Joseph is mentioned. These have become known as the Seven Sorrows of St. Joseph—paralleling the seven swords that the prophet Simeon predicted would pierce Mary's heart.

Over time, it became a pious practice to pair the Seven Sorrows with the Seven Joys of St. Joseph that fill out the rest of each biblical story. With those additions, the faithful are able to see the saint's life more completely; he is understood to be not a silent sufferer but a quiet and devoted man of God who experienced the fullness of life, with all its challenges and all its happiness. He was a person very much like all of us.

Whatever the roots of this devotion, it has long endured in various iterations, prayed by individuals or in groups. And the revered figure behind it all continues to capture our imaginations and deserve our veneration.

In 2020, Pope Francis declared a Year of St. Joseph to be observed beginning on December 8 of that year. The Holy Father wrote: "Each of us can discover in Joseph—the man who goes unnoticed, a daily, discreet and hidden presence—an intercessor, a support, and a guide in times of trouble. Saint Joseph reminds us that those who appear hidden or in the shadows can play an incomparable role in the history of salvation."[1]

Yes, Joseph is the official patron of the Universal Church, of workers, fathers, expectant mothers, families, carpenters, realtors, immigrants, laborers, cemetery workers, happy deaths, and so much more. (A rough tally counts more than forty-five other patronages!) But I think his role is yet greater than all of that. Joseph is a man for us all and a saint to walk with us and bring us courage.

From all of these threads, this little book you now hold in your hands was woven together. It is a work of reflection, contemplation, prayer, and hope. I hope it helps you befriend this saint in new and life-affirming ways.

WHY PRAY WITH ST. JOSEPH?

- *Joseph is the patron for all of us who want to learn how to listen.* Joseph has no lines in the Bible; there is no "Magnificat" attributed to him, no prayer, no words of wisdom, no catchy quotes. Instead, he is famous for his silence. He is most notable for what he heard and did. He listened. He dreamed. He waited. He followed the advice of angels. He went where God led him. Joseph is a figure of holy trust. He teaches us that silence is golden—and that the quiet ones, the shy ones, can sometimes change the world.

- *Joseph is the patron of all who need to learn how to trust in God.* "Let go and let God" could have been his motto. Faced with an unexpected pregnancy and the possibility of scandal, he trusted God's will, cared for the woman he loved, and protected the child she bore.

- *Joseph is the patron of those who end up being sent where they may not want to go.* Joseph had to travel with his pregnant wife to Bethlehem, then flee to Egypt, then return to Nazareth, and then retrace his steps in Jerusalem when it seemed his son was lost. In so many ways, he is a patron for all who might be fearful about the future, and for all who are forced to go a difficult and dangerous way. Joseph is an intercessor and protector for refugees, for migrants, for soldiers. And he stands before God's throne for anyone who is anxious or worried about what is coming. In so many ways, he is a saint for our anxious times.

- *Joseph is the patron for all who feel unworthy or unready.* He was chosen for an extraordinary role in salvation history. Scripture describes him as "righteous." There is no doubt he was a good and holy man. But how could he possibly have been ready to be the earthly father of the Son of God? Joseph was a man with courage enough to surrender himself to the will of God, ready to become what God intended him to be. What did that take? Patience. Attention. Trust. Prayer. He did it by having faith in times of uncertainty and courage in times of doubt. These are qualities each of us needs in our own troubled and often anxious times, and in our ordinary, everyday lives. I sometimes think that when we are facing a seemingly insurmountable problem, we should ask ourselves, "What would Joseph do?" He's a saint for all of us.

In a world where so many families are more dysfunctional than holy, more broken than whole, we might find help and hope by asking for advice from the silent partner of the Holy Family, that other carpenter from Nazareth. The quiet member of the Holy Family has much to say, if we are willing to listen. The one who taught Jesus to measure and cut and build can teach us too how to measure our days, cut off what is unneeded, and craft lives of faith that can endure.

HOW TO USE THIS BOOK

This book is designed for personal reading and reflection. You won't find a lot of heady theology or arcane translations from

Greek. It is intended to spark ideas and stir the imagination. I know working on this book has stirred my own imagination, as I've sought to offer insights about the life and challenges of one of the Church's most beloved saints, a man venerated in virtually every Catholic church in the world—but a man about whom we know very little. Portions of this book dip into what may have been his own imagination, thoughts, and dreams in an attempt to help us understand him better and see him as a man in full.

This book includes two short appendices that offer additional ways to connect with St. Joseph. The first includes a variety of traditional and contemporary prayers to St. Joseph. The second appendix offers a format for praying the Seven Sorrows Devotion in a small group setting, which can be used as part of a novena, a retreat, or as a regular prayer for men's groups or families.

May this powerful saint be a source of inspiration and hope to us all and walk with us as we journey forward, recalling his sorrows and joys as we confront and embrace the sorrows and joys of our own lives.

St. Joseph, pray for us!

Deacon Greg Kandra
May 1, 2021
Feast of St. Joseph the Worker

1.

JOSEPH DECIDES TO DIVORCE MARY

A Matter of Trust

Now this is how the birth of Jesus Christ came about. When his mother Mary was betrothed to Joseph, but before they lived together, she was found with child through the holy Spirit. Joseph her husband, since he was a righteous man, yet unwilling to expose her to shame, decided to divorce her quietly.

Matthew 1:18–19

WALK WITH JOSEPH

It wasn't supposed to be like this. When Joseph dreamed of his life with the young woman named Mary, he could not have imagined that there could possibly be anyone else. But now she was expecting a child? How could this be?

Arriving at his shop early in the morning, when the skies were still dark and lamplight scattered shadows around the planks and sawdust and tools, he saw all the unfinished work he had yet to do. But there was not just the work with wood that was incomplete. What about the marriage plans, their future together? People would talk. It would be a scandal. This girl who had seemed to him, to everyone, the model of purity and piety, now with child. What was going on? Did she love someone else?

For days, Joseph agonized. When did this happen? She seemed so innocent, so trusting, so faithful and steadfast. Was it an illusion? Had it all been a mistake? A misunderstanding?

Pray one Our Father and one Hail Mary and meditate on Joseph's story.

How often do we wonder if we have misread or misjudged a situation? How often do we think we've made a terrible mistake, and we just want to fix it and make it right? So many times we worry about just what "making it right" means, and what it means to do the right thing. How can we know?

From the first moments we meet him in scripture, Joseph, the man destined to be the earthly father of Jesus, is plagued with problems. The greatest story ever told doesn't begin smoothly. There is mystery and uncertainty, doubt, and whisperings of divorce. Scandal is in the air. We're never told just how he learned of Mary's condition or the circumstances that led him to believe that the only option was a quiet divorce. But we can imagine the news left him feeling sad and confused—possibly even betrayed. He surely would have been anxious. Joseph is a man beset with problems. And for good reason.

In ancient Judaism, betrothal was essentially the same as marriage, even though a couple might not be living together. Breaking it off would have signaled to the world—or, at least, the neighbors in Nazareth—that something had gone horribly wrong.

For centuries, theologians have puzzled over just what Joseph knew and when; like so many elements of the saint's life, scripture is silent on the question. Some writers suggest that his faith was so deep that he somehow knew that this child was of the Holy Spirit, and he wanted to end the relationship with Mary out of fear. Pope Benedict XVI, among others, has written that he thinks that Joseph suspected the worst and feared that Mary had broken their engagement. Joseph thus needed to be reassured by an angel that all would be well.

Benedict writes in *Jesus of Nazareth*, "After the discovery that Joseph made, his task was to interpret and apply the law correctly. He does so with love: He does not want to give Mary up to public shame. He wishes her well, even in the hour of his great disappointment."[2] We have no magisterial teaching about what motivated Joseph to end his betrothal to Mary. It remains a mystery. But in the middle of this mystery, we get a glimpse into the man who will serve as the earthly father to God's Son.

Among the many extraordinary details of Jesus's entrance into human history—amid the angels and miracles and awe—we meet someone so very much like us. It binds him not only to the human reality that the Christ child will face but also to generations of us who will follow Jesus and call ourselves Christian. We see in this tender and worried figure a father, a worker, an ordinary man thrust into extraordinary circumstances. He's one of us.

We also see a man whose best-laid plans and most beautiful dreams have suddenly and astoundingly been dashed. Here, we meet someone whose ambitions and hopes are not only thwarted—they are twisted into something he could never have imagined. What he must have felt was more than disappointment. It was heartbreak.

Joseph was a man destined to play a singular role in human history, and it may well have all begun with immense, soul-crushing sorrow.

———

Bent over his bench, Joseph worried. He worried for her. He worried about her. He worried about the child, from an unknown and unnamed father. Who did this? What would she do? What should he do?

Anxiety became grief as he saw so clearly that the life he had imagined—a life with her, a life with a growing family, a life of quiet Sabbaths and family weddings and, eventually, grandchildren playing in his shop, a life saturated in the simple pleasures of a carpenter in a small town—would never come to pass. It was done. It was dead.

"Forget it," a voice told him. "Forget her. There are other women. Be patient. You'll find another. Or maybe you'll be better off alone, free, unshackled." He would think that way sometimes, and something would catch in his throat and it was all he could do to keep from weeping. "Poor old Joseph," they'd be saying one day, long after others in the town had married and raised children and watched them grow into adulthood. And they'd see him alone and speculate "Whatever happened to that girl Mary? What went wrong? They seemed so happy."

After all the sleeplessness and worry and wonder, hours spent planning how to work out a divorce so that Mary would not be subjected to gossip, he fell into bed one night and slipped into a deep, enveloping sleep. But it didn't last.

Such was his intention when, behold, the angel of the Lord appeared to him in a dream and said, "Joseph, son of David, do not be afraid to take Mary your wife into your home. For it is through the holy Spirit that this child has been conceived in her. She will bear a son and you are to name him Jesus, because he will save his people from their sins." All this took place to fulfill what the Lord had said through the prophet:

"Behold, the virgin shall be with child and
    bear a son,
and they shall name him Emmanuel,"

which means "God is with us." When Joseph awoke, he did as the angel of the Lord had commanded him and took his wife into his home. He had no relations with her until she bore a son, and he named him Jesus. (Mt 1:20–25)

Was this what he was meant to do all along? As Joseph put together the pieces of his life, he could feel his heart pounding in his chest. As a carpenter would, he habitually measured and sized things up, to see how they might fit together; to see what new plan he could create. God was calling him to do something incredible. Could that really be true? The dream had been so clear. He couldn't ignore it.

When he awoke the next morning, he knew what he had to do. The first light broke over the horizon. He heard the sounds of voices, the chatter of women heading to the well, and children being fed. Nazareth was the same as always. But everything was different. The world had changed. Joseph had changed. And that anxious pounding in his chest slowly gave way to something he could not even have anticipated the night before—excitement, exhilaration, joy.

———•———

We don't know if Joseph was given to wild and extravagant dreams, or if this was just the first time an angel came to visit and give advice. Maybe it had happened before. Joseph may have had a mystical streak—he had the blood of kings and prophets coursing through his veins—but for whatever reason, at this moment, in the middle of a dark night of the soul, he saw light.

Joseph didn't just see it. He heard it—the amazing news that God had shown Mary favor, that he need not fear, for the Lord was with him—with them both. He took this seriously, accepted that this was not an accident. Joseph was a man who trusted. More important, he believed. He must have believed that God had something planned for his life and so he surrendered everything—his anxiety, his suspicions, his doubts—and chose, during a moment of uncertainty, to make a decision.

He chose to let go and let God lead. Could any of us do as much?

So often we make choices from a place of fear. I can't relocate. I can't quit my job. I can't get married. The timing is wrong. The circumstances aren't right. The risks are too great, the dangers too real, the pitfalls too terrifying. But do we ever seek out a second opinion? Do we ever ask God, "What should I do? Speak, Lord. Your servant is listening."

The simple fact is that Joseph did all that and more. He trusted mystery. He believed a dream. He took what for so many of us would have been an impossible leap of faith. That choice, his yes, gave God a home on earth—a dwelling place where salvation history could unfold.

One of the great questions for each of us is: What do we do when life doesn't go the way we planned? How do we face disappointment, pain, thwarted hopes or ambitions? How do we trust God's hand when he seems to be rewriting or redirecting the story of our lives? We might begin by looking to Joseph.

A priest once told me when I was in formation, "God has a dream for you. Your job is to figure out what it is." How do we do that? We begin by asking him to guide us. And then we ask him to open our hearts to be ready to dream. We need to be ready to listen to angels, to let God enter our lives in unexpected ways. Otherwise we aren't really building or creating or continuing God's work on earth. We're just sawing wood and hammering nails.

Pray for an answer to the great, haunting question of life: How is God calling you to make something new? Pray for the courage you need to trust and say, "Yes, Lord."

REFLECT

In which circumstances of my life do I have a hard time trusting?

What do I think has caused me to be untrusting in those situations?

When have I heard or felt God urging me toward a difficult change? How did I respond?

Did my response draw me closer to God?

What can I do this week to help me become more trusting?

PRAY

Holy Joseph,
you lived the simple and predictable life of a carpenter,
planning and building, dreaming and praying.
Yet you saw God take the clean lines and sharp angles of an
ordinary life
and bend them with his perfect hand.

Righteous Joseph,
God chose you, just as he chose Mary,
to help bring his Son into the world.
Through the mysterious beauty of a dream,
you said yes to God's will,
yes to accepting a role unrivaled in human history,
yes to being the guardian of God's most precious treasure,
and the father of humanity's hope.

Trusting Joseph,
when I receive news I never wanted to hear,
help me to open myself to God's will.
comfort me in my fear, console me in my anxiety,
and remind me in this fallen world of God's never-failing
grace.

Patient Joseph,
teach me to trust as you trusted,
to believe when I doubt, to hope when I despair,
and to follow the voices of angels.
Help me every day to live as you lived,
with trust in God that ultimately brings true joy.
I ask this through the source of your joy,
the one you loved as your own son, Jesus Christ.
Amen.

2.

JOSEPH SEES JESUS BORN INTO POVERTY

A Father's Despair

Joseph too went up from Galilee from the town of Nazareth to Judea, to the city of David that is called Bethlehem, because he was of the house and family of David, to be enrolled with Mary, his betrothed, who was with child. While they were there, the time came for her to have her child, and she gave birth to her firstborn son. She wrapped him in swaddling clothes and laid him in a manger, because there was no room for them in the inn.

Luke 2:4–7

WALK WITH JOSEPH

The journey had been long, much longer than he thought it would be. But this had been a time of shocks and surprises. The joy of a new life, a new marriage, a new family had quickly given way to uncertainty and a gnawing feeling of unworthiness. He wasn't ready. He wasn't prepared. He wasn't wise enough or smart enough or rich enough or holy enough to be the husband he needed to be or the father it seemed God was asking him to be. His waking moments became a living prayer, really more like a pleading: "God, help me!"

And then Joseph and Mary found themselves on the road to Bethlehem, just as his son was about to come into the world. Walking the route he knew so well—he'd been there often as a young man—he recognized landmarks, places he remembered. He thought of family he'd known but lost touch with, friends who had moved on. His thoughts raced. What would his life be like a few weeks from now, after the child was born? As they walked on, he looked up at the stars—wondering, imagining, worrying. He heard the quiet clop-clop-clop of the donkey as it made its way, Mary on its back, her small hands clutching the withers as she struggled to stay awake. Joseph saw the clouds that were gathering. Would it rain?

On the night they arrived, Joseph again faced what he had not expected: the innkeeper standing at the door, candlelight flickering behind him, telling him he had no more rooms. Joseph pleaded. "My wife . . ." he began, but couldn't find the words. He gestured helplessly toward the woman on the donkey.

The innkeeper looked over Joseph's shoulder and saw what was obvious. She was pregnant, tired, and clearly uncomfortable. He nodded, waving his hand. "Behind the house," he said. "There's space in the back. The stable."

And no sooner had he helped his wife from the donkey than she clasped her husband's hand. "It's time," she whispered. "He's coming."

Just a few hours later, as a light rain fell and the animals in the yard ate their feed and stomped their hooves, as the smell of hay and manure and damp wood mingled with the aroma of sweat, the child was born. When it was over, Joseph surveyed the scene with wonder and relief—but also with a quiet feeling of failure. It wasn't supposed to be this way. Mary gave birth on the ground, on the donkey's blanket, amid straw and mud, and his child had no real roof over his head—rainwater dripped down from gaps in the roof—and no real cradle for a bed. Mary laid him in the only empty space she could find, the manger. He lay on scraps of cloth atop straw and grain and dust.

But in the middle of it all, Joseph looked up at the sky he glimpsed between the broken slats of the stable roof. The rain became a drizzle. He caught sight of the stars again. And he quietly gave thanks to God. They were safe, for now, and warm. They could rest.

But his first hours as a father were spent with his family in the land of his ancestors—not in a palace fit for a king but in a shed surrounded by livestock. Joseph took it all in and felt the soft rain splash against his head, trickling down his face, and he tasted in that moment his own tears.

Pray one Our Father and one Hail Mary and meditate on Joseph's story.

It happens so often. When I celebrate the Sacrament of Baptism and I ask parents, "What do you ask of God's Church for your child?," someone will answer, "Happiness!" Sometimes a parent will say, "Peace" or "A good life." (The correct answer, if you're wondering, is "Baptism.") I never fail to be touched by the sincerity and joy contained in those answers. Parents want the best for their children—they want lives without hardship or conflict or need. They want to spare them the messiness and pain that is an inevitable part of living.

And I imagine that is what Joseph wanted for his son: "Happiness!" He wanted the child to know security, safety, protection. He wanted to spare him from hunger and cold, from hardship and difficulty. He would do anything to make that happen.

But there he was, in a strange and uncomfortable place, far from the people he knew, without a home, watching as the most precious child in human history came into the world amid mud and manure, with no bed to sleep in and no family or caregivers to welcome him beyond his mother and father. Joseph watched it all with a sense of sadness and shame. God had chosen him, Joseph, for an extraordinary role, and in the very first moments of fatherhood, he was failing.

Or was he? For all the human sorrow he felt at the way Jesus came into the world, Joseph must have also felt a sense of surrender and, perhaps, peace. God had brought him to that place, to that moment. It was his will, wasn't it? Surely, this was playing out the way God intended.

What happened in an unremarkable corner of the world on an utterly unremarkable night would leave an indelible mark on history. But it occurred with such simplicity and humility, amid the creatures that were made to bear burdens and work and serve. There was a quiet beauty in the way this fragile child came into the world. And for that, and for so much more, Joseph could only give thanks to God.

In moments of mystery, when life seems to have taken a turn we never anticipated, we can do no less. When we have done our best but feel we have failed, we need to trust that God is in charge, that he will right what seems wrong, that he will make from the mess of life something beautiful. We must pray, "Thy will be done."

Sometimes, too, the only answer is gratitude. For everything. God is in it all. Everything. The glow of stars, the smell of the earth, the miracle of life.

———

> Now there were shepherds in that region living in the fields and keeping the night watch over their flock. The angel of the Lord appeared to them and the glory of the Lord shone around them, and they were struck with great fear. The angel said to them, "Do not be afraid; for behold, I proclaim to you good news of great joy that will be for all the people. For today in the city of David a savior has been born for you who is Messiah and Lord. And this will be a sign for you: you will find an infant wrapped in swaddling clothes and lying in a manger." And suddenly there was a multitude of the heavenly host with the angel, praising God and saying:
>
> > "Glory to God in the highest
> > and on earth peace to those on whom his
> > favor rests." (Lk 2:8–14)

Joseph watched them sleeping, the mother and child, and in the stillness of that moment he got up and went to the door of the stable. He looked up. The air had cooled. The clouds had vanished. The stars flickered. He made his way into the alley behind the inn and followed a path to the field beyond. He saw sheep grazing. Some were sleeping. He thought he noticed mothers with young lambs, and he smiled. In the distance, he could make out shepherds, talking among themselves, gesturing in the dark.

And in the quiet stillness of that moment, in the ordinariness of the men in the fields and the animals gnawing at threads of grass and the stars spread across a dark sky, it hit him. Something immeasurably beautiful had happened that night. Joseph couldn't describe it. He couldn't put it into words. But he sensed it. He felt it. He believed it. This child sleeping just a few feet away, who had come into the world in such an unlikely and miraculous way, this child's destiny was entwined with human history. God had sent him into this fraction of time, into this plain and broken and unwelcoming place, amid humble animals and poor shepherds and a carpenter who couldn't even give him a proper birthplace, and it had happened this way for some reason that Joseph couldn't yet understand. He couldn't explain it, but he just knew God was at work in this. He had been brought to this place by faith and trust and a dream. What was God planning?

The wind picked up. The trees stirred. Things, he realized, had changed. He closed his eyes and he could hear it. It carried in the air. It was the echo of a voice that had spoken to him in a dream. In a moment, he felt something that had eluded him all evening. Overwhelming peace. Reassurance. Joy.

He smiled and looked again at the sky and whispered, "Thank you." His heart racing, he turned and made his way back toward Mary and Jesus, listening to the sounds of the wind and the murmurings of the sheep and the chatter of the shepherds, and it all sounded to him like music, glorious music.

Are we able to understand, as Joseph seemed to, that the ordinary is really extraordinary? Are we able to see beauty in surprising places? Are we able to trust that, even when things go wrong, God is still at work in our lives?

At this moment in his journey, Joseph may have wondered if the God who had called him to this great adventure had somehow abandoned him. Was the miracle of Jesus really destined to begin in mud and manure? Something had to be wrong. But Joseph, with faith and patience, with prayer and profound trust, was able to realize that something, in fact, was exactly right. Despite impossible circumstances and improbable challenges, a glorious new life had come into the world. Despite the darkness of the night, it was ablaze with stars. Light had come.

Parents never want their children to begin life the way Jesus did. Husbands don't want their wives to endure what the mother of Jesus had to face. Seeing how it unfolded, Joseph couldn't help but feel inadequate and weak, frustrated and alone. But Joseph's disappointment and despair at seeing how Jesus was born could not last. He came to know the "thrill of hope" that came into the world on that night. His experience reminds us that at times when we may feel feeble, God does not see us that way. We are loved. God has plans. He has ideas, a vision, and more hope than we can even imagine.

Look to the stars. And trust. Even in circumstances that seem impossible, the story of Joseph reminds us of all that is possible when we give our lives over in faith to the God of love.

REFLECT

When have I felt disappointed with my life or with things that are beyond my control?

What do I pray when I feel anxious or sad?

What lessons have I learned when I've faced unexpected problems and turned to God for help?

Every experience, even a failure, can be a lesson. How often have I looked for growth in faith during times of setback or disappointment?

What can I do today to face life with stronger faith, clearer hope, and deeper trust?

PRAY

Searching Joseph,
you journeyed far to seek shelter and security in
Bethlehem,
only to find instead a place that had no room
for the Savior of the world.
I can only imagine the disappointment and heartbreak
you felt watching the Son of God come into the world
as a pauper—with no true home,
and little shelter from the elements and the hardships of
life.

Anxious Joseph,
the sorrow you felt is the sorrow of every parent
dreaming of a good life for their children

and often wishing things could be better than they are.
But your steadfastness and faith remind us:
Trust always in God's tender mercy!
Give thanks to him in all circumstances,
believe in his plan, pray for his guidance,
ask for his consolation and strength.

Hopeful Joseph,
help me to gaze toward God in the darkest of nights,
and see the stars.
Teach me how to count my blessings,
numbering God's miracles in my own life,
with humility and steadiness and faith.
May I always see in your example
a model of quiet confidence:
an example of fidelity and strength.
I ask this in the name of your son, Jesus,
who came into an unwelcoming world
to bring all of us a sense of welcome,
possibility, and hope.
Amen.

3.

JOSEPH SORROWS AT THE CIRCUMCISION OF JESUS

A Father's Compassion

When eight days were completed for his circumcision, he was named Jesus, the name given him by the angel before he was conceived in the womb.

Luke 2:21

WALK WITH JOSEPH

For all the challenges of the last few weeks—the journey to Bethlehem, the birth of the child, the problems of caring for a newborn in such barren, primitive conditions—there was one important task that was not difficult: finding a mohel to perform a circumcision.

Bethlehem—tiny, crowded, overwhelmed with people arriving for the census—had no shortage of holy men available for the ritual. Joseph made some inquiries and was directed to a small home off a meandering alley, where a knock on the door led him to an elderly man with tired, sympathetic eyes. "Bring the boy here," he whispered.

And so the next day, Joseph took the child to formally make him a part of the tradition that had been handed on through his family for centuries. He had considered this a cherished and beautiful testament of faith. But at the moment of circumcision, when the blade pierced the boy's flesh and he let out a sudden, anguished cry, Joseph found himself fighting back tears. He closed his eyes, whispered a prayer, and his mind raced.

He imagined the cuts, pains, bruises this boy would suffer as he grew up—the falls, the missteps, the accidents of life. The cry of this child was a sign of life—but also a reminder of suffering and hardship. What would he have to endure? Joseph wondered. He opened his eyes to see the mohel cleaning his blade, the cloth now stained with fresh bright blood.

Pray one Our Father and one Hail Mary and meditate on Joseph's story.

It is one thing to hear a child cry from hunger or discomfort or simply the need to make a noise. It's something else when the cry is from severe physical pain—the shedding of blood. What parent doesn't feel that pain in their own heart? What compassionate person doesn't feel that sting?

Joseph could only watch in anguish and quiet empathy as the child he'd tried so carefully to protect and care for faced the first brutal reality of human life: it is a life that comes with pain.

It is likely that, across his life, Joseph attended a number of rites of *Brit Milah*, circumcision; it was a part of his upbringing, his culture, his family, his faith. He probably witnessed the circumcisions of members of his own family. If, as we know some speculate, he had been a widower, with grown children, perhaps he watched another son be circumcised.

Scripture, of course, is silent about whatever life Joseph had before his relationship with Mary. But when counting the sorrows of Joseph's life, surely hearing the cry of the newborn Jesus as he was circumcised ranks among the most personal and most painful. Here, a covenant was being fulfilled and a promise kept; but here, too, a beloved child was experiencing the harsh reality of human pain.

While this small but significant moment in history gets only a passing mention in the gospels, it's not hard to imagine that it was seared into Joseph's heart. And it carries deeper meaning for us now. In the first days of Jesus's earthly life, we see a foreshadowing of how that life will end, with flesh pierced and blood spilled. The cry of the newborn joins the cry of the crucified—*Eli, Eli, lema sabachthani?* "My God, my God, why have you forsaken me?" (Mt 27:46) —to remind us that the Suffering Servant came into the world as one of us, flesh and blood, fully embracing our humanity and sharing our pain. As we pray in Eucharistic Prayer IV, Jesus "shared our human nature in all things but sin."

St. Joseph bore witness to that intimately. He was among the first to see the Son of God bleed, to hear him cry out in pain, and watch as he submitted himself to the law to fulfill a covenant. Joseph may well not have lived to witness the unbearable agony of his son's Crucifixion, but he surely knew something of the torment parents know when they have to watch a child's agony.

––•––

Within moments, it was over. But not completely. There was one more act to be carried out. The mohel gently placed the boy into Joseph's arms. The boy fidgeted and squirmed but settled when he looked up at his father. Joseph felt a shiver and thought at first it was the baby, but then realized the nervous trembling was his own.

His son's eyes fixed on Joseph's face. There was recognition. Assurance. Comfort. And then in the midst of a prayer of blessing, the mohel paused and pronounced the boy's name: "Yeshua." Jesus. This was the first time Joseph had heard someone outside the family say it. It caught him off guard. Suddenly, incredibly, what the angel had foretold was all very real and true. Jesus—the name spoken in a dream; the name Mary had shared with him when she talked about the child. The name Joseph understood to be ordained by God. The name of a rescuer. A savior.

The mohel spoke it again, touching the child on his head. "Yeshua," he said with a smile. He looked at Joseph. "He has a good, loud cry. He's not shy. You won't have to wonder if he will be heard."

Then Joseph smiled. He held in his arms a tiny rescuer—but one who could clearly make a lot of noise. With a voice like that, what would he be? "I hope he doesn't wake up the neighbors," Joseph said to the mohel.

Joseph could barely contain himself. What had begun months ago on a mysterious night with a vivid dream had become, at that moment, fulfilled, and Joseph looked with wonder and joy at a miracle he could barely comprehend, sleeping in his arms.

———

St. Paul wrote to the people of Philippi, "At the name of Jesus, every knee should bend" (Phil 2:10). While this brief passage from Luke's gospel doesn't tell us how Joseph (or anyone else) reacted to hearing the name of Jesus proclaimed publicly—possibly for the first time—it nonetheless strikes a chord. Something is beginning.

Think of all the times the name of Jesus has been pronounced from pulpits, chanted in prayers, evoked in speeches, proclaimed to both believers and unbelievers across the centuries. Think of where that name has been spoken: in cathedrals and humble huts, in classrooms and church basements, in barrooms and at Bible camps. It's spoken with love and with loathing, as a cry and a curse. It is a name recognized and acknowledged by billions. It is a name that has literally traveled the world. But here it is, at the very beginning.

Joseph, hearing it, hears a prophesy fulfilled, a promise granted. All because of a name. This isn't a name he or his wife selected. It was chosen for the child, as part of a divine plan. At this moment, something miraculous is happening. Joseph may not quite understand it, he may not quite grasp the significance—or how the course of history would be changed by that name—but his heart is deeply moved. After the pain of witnessing his child's circumcision, with the desperate cry of his new son, he knows a moment of incalculable joy, a gift of grace.

REFLECT

When I encounter the suffering of another, do I see the face of Christ?

How do I respond to someone in pain—whether physical, emotional, spiritual?

How has God come to my aid and alleviated my suffering?

What do St. Joseph's compassion and sacrifice teach me about love?

PRAY

Compassionate Joseph,
you loved the Son of God as if he were your own flesh and blood,
suffering with him and sharing every pain of his young life,
shedding tears of sorrow at his circumcision when he cried out.

Comforting Joseph,
you cradled the baby Jesus with a father's love,
wiping away every tear,
with tenderness and strength,
using the strong, calloused hands of a carpenter
to console and caress and calm.

Giving Joseph,
you gave such care to the Son of God,
as you heard the cries that foretold the suffering of Calvary
and the redemption of our world.

Hear my prayers this day.
Be my inspiration, my consolation, and my guide.
Help my heart to be more caring,
guide my hands to be more gentle,
and whenever I feel the pains and pangs of life,
remind me that I am not alone,
but that you are by my side,
just as you were with your son, Jesus.
Amen.

4.

JOSEPH HEARS A PREDICTION OF SUFFERING

A Husband's Anguish

When the days were completed for their purification according to the law of Moses, they took him up to Jerusalem to present him to the Lord, just as it is written in the law of the Lord, "Every male that opens the womb shall be consecrated to the Lord," and to offer the sacrifice of "a pair of turtledoves or two young pigeons," in accordance with the dictate in the law of the Lord.

Now there was a man in Jerusalem whose name was Simeon. This man was righteous and devout, awaiting the consolation of Israel, and the holy Spirit was upon him. It had been revealed to him by the holy Spirit that he should not see death before he had seen the Messiah of the Lord. He

came in the Spirit into the temple; and when the
parents brought in the child Jesus to perform the
custom of the law in regard to him, he took him
into his arms and blessed God, saying:

> "Now, Master, you may let your servant go
>   in peace, according to your word,
> for my eyes have seen your salvation,
>   which you prepared in sight of all the peoples,
> a light for revelation to the Gentiles
>   and glory for your people Israel."

The child's father and mother were amazed at
what was said about him; and Simeon blessed them
and said to Mary his mother, "Behold, this child
is destined for the fall and rise of many in Israel,
and to be a sign that will be contradicted (and you
yourself a sword will pierce) so that the thoughts of
many hearts may be revealed."

Luke 2:22–35

WALK WITH JOSEPH

*For the first time since the baby was born, Mary and Joseph left the
relative safety and security of Bethlehem and the daily routine they
had gotten used to, and the three of them ventured to Jerusalem:
Mary on the donkey, cradling Jesus in her arms, Joseph walking beside
them, leading them along the road. Joseph felt the usual anxiety—
worrying, constantly worrying. Had they packed enough? Was the
journey going to be too long, too difficult? Were they rushing things?
Was this a mistake?*

*But he had followed the law and the customs this far; God
had guided and protected them. "Just trust," he told himself. "Just*

trust. The Lord will provide." They traveled most of the way in silence, sometimes praying, sometimes singing, sometimes stopping to change the baby's clothes or let him nurse. A few times, they stopped to draw water from a well. At moments like these, Joseph found himself watching in wonder at this small, miraculous family that had come into his life—seeing his wife's smile, stroking his son's hair as the boy's eyes closed and he fell asleep. Serenity. Quiet. Hope. Joseph felt all these things and could not imagine ever being more content. His life up until now had been well ordered and simple. Working with wood, constructing something new out of nothing, putting pieces together—all that gave him a sense of satisfaction and accomplishment. But this? This was something altogether different and new.

In time, the road became a street and they passed more people and heard the rumbling of wagons and the chatter of tourists. And then there it was: the high wall, the crowded buildings, smoke rising from fires and ovens and offerings. Jerusalem.

They made their way under the gate, the donkey clop-clopping on the hard pavement. They arrived at the Temple and were directed to a side door. Joseph found the place for the donkey and offered a small coin to the boy tending the animals. He helped Mary to the ground, the baby fussing in her arms, and just moments later, they were inside.

It was unexpectedly cool, but the air was thick with smoke, incense, the aroma from candles and charcoal and wood and the mingled stench of dirt and sickness and perfume and sweat. The poor and the lame were huddled against the wall near the door. They watched the family as they stepped into the Temple. Joseph caught sight of a hand in the crowd reaching out, and a stranger's pained face, his mouth trying to form a word.

Joseph looked anxiously around for someone who could give them direction and glimpsed an elderly man in a far corner, watching them intently. He looked helpful. Joseph headed in his direction, and then saw the old man nodding and coming toward him.

The old man's walk was labored and slow. But his eyes focused on the child. Joseph soon had second thoughts and stopped in his tracks. He and Mary exchanged glances, but then the old man was there, right in front of them. His eyes darted from Joseph to Mary and then rested on Jesus. He took a deep breath and closed his eyes and extended a hand and whispered an ancient blessing.

"My name is Simeon," he told them, "and I've been waiting for you." Simeon nodded toward the baby. "I've been waiting for him." Joseph was convinced the man must be mad. Then Simeon began to speak and couldn't stop. He spoke of prophecies being fulfilled, of destinies being revealed. He looked at the slumbering Jesus with a mixture of wonder, fear, and awe. He reached out to touch his head, then stopped and his eyes went to Mary. He closed them for a long moment. "Your heart will be broken," he whispered. He opened his eyes and gazed at her intently. "You will feel yourself pierced by a sword." He shook his head wearily. "It has to be this way."

Mary flinched. She began to move away. Joseph pulled her back, drew her close to him, and struggled to say something. But then the old man looked at him and grabbed his arm. Then Simeon loosened his grip, his voice became soft, even reassuring. Joseph saw a tear in his eye and the old man said, "You will understand one day."

Pray one Our Father and one Hail Mary and meditate on Joseph's story.

Joseph was a man of profound obedience and strict fidelity. He did as the law prescribed and, again and again, went where God led him. So it was that, just a few weeks after the baby's birth, his family made the journey to Jerusalem. The biblical commentator William Barclay noted the Jewish law of the day: "When a woman had borne a child, if it was a boy, she was unclean for forty days; if it was a girl, for eighty days. She could go about her household and her daily business, but she could not enter the temple or share in any religious ceremony (Leviticus 12)."[3] At the end of that time, she would go to the Temple to make a sacrifice.

The sacrifice itself is telling, Barclay explains; a pigeon was considered an offering of the poor. Barclay sees this as another sign of the humble circumstances into which Jesus was born. In fact, by the standards of the day, this little family was more than holy; it was also poor.

Still, Joseph and Mary did what was commanded of them—and made every effort to follow both the letter and spirit of the law. So we can imagine the shock, then sadness, that they felt when a stranger, the aged Simeon, encountered them at the Temple and pronounced a prophecy of suffering and pain.

What should have been a moment of excitement, a rite of passage for the new mother and her baby, became instead a warning. Be prepared for heartbreak. Yours will be a life of pain. How did Joseph feel when he heard this? How would any husband and father have felt? He realized the woman he loved would suffer—how or why, he could not imagine. She was so young, so vulnerable; she had endured so much already and had sacrificed so much. What else lay ahead? How could he possibly ease her pain or mend her broken heart?

This was more than just one more hardship to absorb. It was an ominous warning. And it frightened Joseph. He may have felt the odds against them were impossible. After all he had done and tried to do for her, for the baby, for their new life together, it was not enough to shield them from the cruelty of living. What else could he do? He could pray. Have faith. Hope. But was that enough?

When we receive news we don't want to hear, a diagnosis we didn't expect, a twist in the road that takes us where we never wanted to go, we can remember Joseph. We can remember and find courage in his stoicism and his strength. We can remember his trust and his faith and find hope.

Through everything that God gave him—every burden, problem, difficulty—Joseph stood fast. He didn't flinch when the Lord added to the weight he was carrying.

He shows us a way—a way of trust, confidence, and quiet strength. He shows us the way of faith.

So many times, Joseph could have just walked away. But he didn't. He couldn't.

This righteous man was a man of his word. His way was one steeped in love and abiding faith.

When it was all done, and the prayers had been said and the offering made, they walked back to begin the return journey, and Joseph could not forget what Simeon had said: "My eyes have seen your salvation . . . and glory for your people Israel."

There was more to the prophet's message than just pain. There was the promise of something extraordinary. "Did you hear what he said?" Joseph whispered.

"I can't think about it," Mary replied. "It's too much." She looked down at the baby sleeping in her arms as they made their way past the beggars and the people selling animals to be offered. She heard the cooing of pigeons and the gentle coughing of lambs and smelled the damp hair and sweat and smoldering incense. It was overwhelming. She felt her stomach turn. "Let's just go," she said. "It's getting late."

The baby stirred and began to fuss and she pulled him close to nurse him. Joseph looked up and scanned the scene outside the Temple: the vendors, the sellers, the parents with children, the rabbis and teachers and students moving slowly, their robes dusting the pavement, their lips moving in silent prayer. The world looked the same as it did before. But everything had changed.

When Mary finished, he helped her up on the donkey. She saw the worry in his eyes.

"Joseph," she said, "remember your dream. Don't be afraid." She smiled and his heart melted; he smiled back and felt his cheeks turn crimson.

They began the journey home, his heart pounding in his chest. He heard again the familiar sound of the donkey's hooves and remembered when he heard that on the way to Bethlehem. It reminded him of the sound of a hammer against wood. Rhythmic. Repetitious. Familiar. For the first time in weeks, he felt calmed, reassured, and even a little excited.

Joseph realized that there was so much more to all of this than he thought. He was being swept up in something larger than he'd imagined. He swallowed hard and whispered a prayer of gratitude. Improbably, incredibly, God had chosen him to be a part of this. His heart swelled. The words of the psalm formed on his lips: "Give thanks to the LORD for he is good. His mercy endures forever!" (Ps 107:1).

He heard Mary's soft voice singing a lullaby to the baby. The afternoon shadows were growing longer. The air was cooling. Joseph smiled. He was overcome with an indescribable joy. Nothing could be more beautiful than this moment, this fraction of time. Whatever would come, God would be with them. He was sure of it now.

———

One of the prayers in the Mass puts it so simply: "We wait in joyful hope for the coming of our Savior, Jesus Christ." In this encounter with Simeon, we see that hope expressed and then realized, as the holy prophet holds in his arms the salvation he has been waiting for.

In this moment, Joseph hears more than a prophecy; he hears history. He could trace his bloodline all the way back to David—that was what brought him to Bethlehem, after all—but in this dramatic interaction in the holiest site of his faith, Jerusalem's Temple, he sees history unfolding before his eyes, "a glory for your people Israel."

The joy of this is more than fatherly pride; it is Joseph's sudden awareness of a prayer being answered, a hope fulfilled. He is told that God has entered human history in the person of this small, helpless baby—the child he's being asked to help raise!—and he realizes that he, Joseph, is part of a larger plan.

We can't know just how much of this Joseph grasped or understood; scripture only tells us he was "amazed" at what he heard. Who wouldn't be? But in his amazement and wonder, we realize our own humility before God's love for us. It's often said that "God writes straight with crooked lines," and so often we find ourselves lost in the scribblings of life—the problems, confusions, setbacks, detours that take us where we never expected.

But God is continually, creatively, and carefully writing our story. This moment with Joseph challenges us to follow our own story with patience, gratitude, and trust, aware that God has something to say to each of us. We all have a part to play in God's plan, and we need to watch for its unfolding—and to wait in joyful hope.

REFLECT

In the times when my life took unexpected twists—how did I respond?

How can I be more like Joseph and accept God's will for me with patience and joy?

PRAY

Listening Joseph,
you went to the Temple in Jerusalem out of obedience and
devotion,
with a generous heart,
full of love for God and for your family.
You heard a prophecy you never expected,
words of salvation and glory—but also of sorrow and pain.

Suffering Joseph,
I can only imagine the anguish and sorrow you felt
on hearing the words of the holy and aged Simeon—
how you worried for the family you loved,
and how you wondered what God had in store.

Steadfast Joseph,
you confronted the uncertainties of the future
with faith, with courage, and with trust,
surrendering to God's holy will
and walking a difficult path with gratitude.
You understood that God had chosen you to help raise his
Son,
and you undertook that role with quiet strength and joyful
hope.

Strong Joseph,
help me to live my life with a sense of surrender and trust,
giving back to God some of what he has given to me.
Teach me to accept any challenge, bear any burden,
and walk any difficult path with the same love, courage,
and sense of purpose as you did.
Help me to stay focused on God's will, not mine,

so that I may face the future without undue fear
and with joy everlasting.
Amen.

5.

JOSEPH FLEES WITH HIS FAMILY TO EGYPT

A Desperate Choice

The angel of the Lord appeared to Joseph in a dream and said, "Rise, take the child and his mother, flee to Egypt, and stay there until I tell you. Herod is going to search for the child to destroy him." Joseph rose and took the child and his mother by night and departed for Egypt. He stayed there until the death of Herod, that what the Lord had said through the prophet might be fulfilled, "Out of Egypt I called my son."

Matthew 2:13–15

WALK WITH JOSEPH

It was early morning when she found him. He'd gotten up before dawn and left their place by the inn and gone off to a quiet spot in a nearby field to pray. He did this so often; it was almost part of his morning routine. Mary got up and checked on the baby and saw that Joseph had gone. She made her way to the doorway and looked out and saw the shepherds with their flocks, and then saw Joseph talking with one of them. He told her that he liked their company. They were laborers, he said. Like him. But they saw things differently. Their lives weren't about building or shaping or creating. They were all about tending. Leading. Caring for something that was alive. Theirs was a different way of life, a different way of living. It fascinated him. And so, in the mornings when he had finished praying, he would seek them out, to hear their stories. It helped give his own life focus.

Mary watched him for a moment, then heard the baby begin to stir and went back inside. A few moments later, Joseph appeared in the doorway. She could tell something was wrong.

"You were up early," she said, rewrapping the cloth around Jesus.

"I couldn't sleep," he explained. "Dreams."

She looked at him intently, waiting for more.

"It was like before," he said. "But . . . I don't know."

She reached out, touched his face. He looked at her and then quickly looked away.

"I think we need to leave. Soon." Then he told her everything. He had heard the same voice, felt the same presence that he'd encountered in the first of the dreams, all those months ago. "It was as real as you are," he told her. He took her hands. She noticed he was sweating.

He tried to sound calm, rational. But it was all a jumble. She could tell he was frightened, worried, overwhelmed. The baby was in danger, he said. Herod wanted him dead. He would do anything to make it happen. They had to go. She swallowed hard, nodded, scanned the small room. They had so little. They could leave quickly.

"We can be back in Nazareth by nightfall," she said. "Or maybe tomorrow."

He shook his head. "We need to leave the country. We need to get as far away from Herod, as quickly as possible."

She searched his face for a clue, an explanation. "Where?"

"You will not believe me."

"Of course I will. I have always believed you. I trust you." She took his face in her hands and locked on his eyes. "I love you."

Joseph took a deep breath. "Egypt," he said.

Pray one Our Father and one Hail Mary and meditate on Joseph's story.

A few months after my wife and I were married, I got a promotion at work and was told I would be transferred from Washington to New York. It was a big move, a big opportunity—and as with any relocation, there were all sorts of complications involved: finding a place to live, figuring out a budget, getting used to a new city, new hours, new everything.

It was a grand adventure at the time, all those years ago, full of possibility and a not inconsiderable risk. We didn't have a clue what we were doing. But compared to what Joseph faced? That was nothing. For Joseph, the decision to leave his homeland, the place of his ancestors, was probably the biggest decision of his life—one demanding courage and conviction. This move was more than a leap of faith. It would change their lives forever. And it happened while he was asleep.

A priest once put it to me this way: "Can you imagine? Would you ever make a decision like that based on a dream?" Honestly? No.

But that is probably true for most of us. We weigh our options, do research, spend time googling opinions, watch YouTube videos, ask friends and family for advice. Most of us don't just wake up one morning and decide to move immediately to another country. To do something like that runs the risk of having people decide you're mad—unbalanced, irrational, crazy.

Maybe people would have said that about Joseph, too. Maybe he worried about what something like this might do to his reputation. His family, and perhaps more so, Mary's family, would think he was irresponsible—or worse, an unfit husband and father. You don't just pack up and leave like that, do you? Well, sometimes you have to.

Joseph had a rare gift of being able to listen—and he listened to what he knew were messages from God. He had an extraordinary capacity to trust—to believe and to accept that someone else was in charge of his life and his destiny. He had an unwavering faith, founded on one simple truth: He was only the carpenter. Someone else was drawing up the plans.

————

They packed up what little they had and left that night. They told no one—terrified that somehow Herod would learn where they had gone. After a few hours, walking in the dark of night, they fell into a comfortable rhythm. For Joseph, it was becoming a familiar routine. He measured his footsteps with the donkey and could gauge how far they could go before they needed to take a break. Every few miles, Mary needed to climb down, walk, stretch, rest. She needed to nurse the baby, change him, bathe him. And Joseph needed time alone, to pray.

They had a little money, enough to last them the trip. Along the way, if necessary, he could pick up work in different towns and villages. He was a tradesman, and a good one, and he knew no one would refuse a new father looking for work.

The journey took almost a week. They found shelter in caves or abandoned sheds. The weather was mild. Evenings were cool. The rain held off for most of the trip. They lived on fruits—dates, figs—goats' milk, water from streams.

Joseph knew one or two people in that part of the world—he was hoping he could make connections with men he had worked with before, and they could help him put down roots. He knew it was wild and improbable—Egypt was not a small place—but he also knew that they weren't walking alone. The Lord was walking with them.

Early one morning, they passed through a small border town and found themselves, at last, in Egypt. Joseph was struck by how much of it seemed like home—but how much of it, too, seemed strange. The woodwork, the buildings, the faces of those he passed on the street—it reminded him of places he had been before, but the colors and textures of everything were new and unfamiliar. As they walked slowly through the village, Mary noticed marble statues outside the buildings. Some had small smoking pots burning before them. She realized, with a shock, that they were idols.

She looked down at the ground, closed her eyes, held her baby close to her breast, whispered a prayer—and then heard a crash as something shattered on the ground. The donkey stopped, bucked,

*stomped. Joseph tried to calm it. Mary said, "Help me down. Let's
take a break."*

*He helped her and the baby down to the ground and then
saw over her shoulder what had happened. A crowd was gathering. People were arguing, pointing, gesturing toward Joseph and
the family. One of the statues had come loose from its niche and
shattered on the ground. Joseph and Mary exchanged a look. He
tightened his grip on the rope leading the donkey and whispered,
"Let's keep walking." Mary nodded.*

*Joseph felt both worried and shocked. There were other people
milling about, he thought. Maybe one of them bumped into it. But
in his mind, there was no mistaking what had actually happened.
When they walked past it, the statue somehow moved, trembled,
fell. He remembered Simeon's words: "This child is destined for the
fall and rise of many . . . "*

<hr>

The flight to Egypt is one of the more dramatic and mysterious
events in the life of the Holy Family. We know little about it and
the gospels provide only a few short sentences. There are no
details about where they lived, or for how long. But Christian
tradition is rich with stories, legends, speculation. To this day,
there are places in Egypt that for centuries have been sites of
devotion and prayer, where tradition holds that the Holy Family
stopped, rested, visited, or lived. Stories have sprung up about
miracles and extraordinary encounters—including one about
the young Jesus meeting his cousin John for the first time in
Egypt.

One compelling story tells of how Egypt's pagan idols fell
from their pedestals when the baby Jesus passed by in his moth-

er's arms. The tradition is so strong and enduring that there are ancient religious paintings and icons that depict the moment. There is, of course, no account of this in the gospels.

But perhaps Joseph felt reassurance and hope when he remembered the words of Simeon and, entering this strange new world, had the faith to believe—to just know in his heart—they were on a journey guided by God. Fleeing a ruthless despot, they would start over, begin again. Here, in a place that once held their people as slaves, they could be free. They could be safe.

The Holy Family's time in Egypt challenges us to wonder not just how they managed to live in a strange and unfamiliar place but how any of us would cope with similar circumstances. After World War II, Pope Pius XII considered the plight of families who had been displaced during the war, and famously named the Holy Family as models for all refugees—icons for families on the run.

Today, while so many seek sanctuary from war, violence, drought, or political upheaval, we can remember that the designation "refugee" applies to all of us. We are people in flight. We seek refuge from sorrow, loneliness, and fear. We seek shelter from an unforgiving world. We want protection from prejudice, injustice, and violence. One of the beautiful messages of the flight to Egypt is that the Holy Family, walking on that long journey, still walks with all of us. They accompany anyone who seeks security, safety, dignity, protection—whether it's physical, emotional, or spiritual. And their great strength—Joseph's guiding force—was trust in God.

Remembering this audacious and daring trip, we pray to Jesus, Mary, and Joseph and ask for the courage to trust in God as we make our own journey through life, as physical or spiritual refugees, seeking shelter and security in God's loving arms.

REFLECT

The Holy Family fled a brutal king to seek safety and security in Egypt. What am I trying to escape in my own life? What am I most afraid of?

What was the hardest decision I've ever had to make? How did prayer help me with that?

How does this journey of Joseph speak to me about trust?

PRAY

> Courageous Joseph,
> you answered the words of an angel
> by setting out toward a foreign land,
> going into the desert of a world you did not know
> to save the child you loved,
> the child who himself was born to save the world.
> Help me in moments of weakness and doubt,
> in times of uncertainty and fear,
> to find the courage to live with faith,
> trusting God to guide my way.
>
> Devoted Joseph,
> be my companion, my guide in the deserts of my own life.
> When I feel lost, give me direction;
> when I despair, give me hope;
> when I feel sorrow, offer me the joy of your friendship.

Sheltering Joseph,
you found a home for Jesus and Mary when they sought refuge.
Lead me where I need to go
when I flee the dangers and difficulties of life.
As once you protected the family you loved,
be my protector and my shelter, so that I may find peace.
May your family be forever my family,
and may they always hold me in their loving embrace.
Amen.

6.

JOSEPH MAKES THE DANGEROUS JOURNEY BACK TO ISRAEL

Going Home

When Herod had died, behold, the angel of the Lord appeared in a dream to Joseph in Egypt and said, "Rise, take the child and his mother and go to the land of Israel, for those who sought the child's life are dead." He rose, took the child and his mother, and went to the land of Israel. But when he heard that Archelaus was ruling over Judea in place of his father Herod, he was afraid to go back there. And because he had been warned in a dream, he departed for the region of Galilee. He went and dwelt in a town called Nazareth, so

that what had been spoken through the prophets
might be fulfilled, "He shall be called a Nazorean."
Matthew 2:19–23

WALK WITH JOSEPH

*The days became weeks, the weeks became months, and before
long the family began to feel more comfortable there. Joseph
took work wherever he could, whenever it was offered. They
shared a small room, part of a house belonging to another
family from Israel. It was cramped, but it was enough. Mary
helped care for the children, and in their playtime, Joseph
showed them how to make small toys from scraps of wood.
Jesus grew and was beginning to walk. During the Sabbath,
they gathered with the small community of observant Jews to
pray and read together, to talk, and to wonder: Was there any
news from home? What about friends, relatives, did anyone
have news to share?*

*Sometimes, travelers and tradesmen passed through the vil-
lage and Joseph heard stories, rumors, and speculation. Herod
was mad; he was sick; he hadn't been seen for weeks. Some said
he'd died. Others heard he'd gone on a rampage, killing young boys
out of fear or for sport.*

*Whatever they knew of Egypt and its customs and its culture,
Joseph was sure of this: it wasn't really home. It wasn't what he
knew and was familiar with. It wasn't the place Mary knew. They
both wanted Jesus to grow up in the land of their families, the land
their ancestors had known and loved for generations. They wanted
him to connect with other relatives and friends. They wanted to be
able to take him to Jerusalem, to meet the scholars of the law, to
see and hear and smell the sensations of the land God had given*

them. They wanted him to be able to literally walk in the footsteps of Abraham, Isaac, and Jacob.

Joseph continued his custom of rising early to pray in a deserted spot. Some mornings, he took Jesus with him. The boy held tight to his father's hand as they walked slowly through the village and found a place by a small stream to sit and to think and to pray and to listen. "The Lord will speak if you listen," Joseph whispered. "Be still. Be quiet. Just listen." And Jesus tilted his head and he listened. His eyes darted from place to place, following anything that moved, looking for small animals or wild birds or a leaf carried on the wind. Mostly, all he heard was water in the stream, heading for places he'd never been to.

Joseph took those moments to close his eyes and pray. He prayed for guidance, for strength, for direction. Where was their life headed? How would he know? Would he ever be able to give his family a proper home? The words of the psalm came to him again and again. "Make known to me your ways, LORD," he prayed. "Teach me your paths" (Ps 25:4).

The answer he sought came to him, as it did so often, deep in his sleep. One night, he awoke with a start. He had heard the voice. It was there, in their room. He looked around. Mary and Jesus were both asleep. All was darkness. He listened. The wind stirred. There was no one else there. He lay back down and stared at the wood slats in the ceiling.

The next morning, he wanted to tell Mary, but he wasn't sure. It seemed so improbable. But was it? While his wife and son still slept, he got up and left their room. He paused at a trough to splash water on his face. He saw one of the Jewish men in the village pass by. The man noticed Joseph and waved, then stopped, and came over to him. They nodded a greeting.

The man asked quietly, "Have you heard?" Then, looking around and leaning closer toward Joseph. "It's Herod. He's dead. It's true. My cousin arrived last night. He works as a stone carver in Jerusalem. He told me he saw the funeral with his own eyes, over a month ago. He helped prepare the tomb."

Joseph blinked in disbelief. His lips parted. He didn't know what to say.

His neighbor nodded. "I know. Incredible, isn't it?" He shook his head and went back to his house.

And Joseph stood there, cold water dripping from his bearded chin, blinking. Yes, he thought. It's incredible. But he had already been told, he just hadn't believed it. He remembered vividly the words he had heard in his dream, the same words he had heard that very morning: "Herod is dead." He also remembered, too, the rest of the message: "Go immediately. Go back to Israel."

Standing by the water, Joseph felt his legs go weak. He grabbed the sides of the trough. With Herod dead, his son would be king. Archelaus was a tyrant, as ruthless as his father. How could he even think of going back? It was madness. And it was terrifying. Joseph dried his hands and face on his robe and started walking back to their room. He turned it all over again and again in his mind—the dream, the voice, the conversation over a trough of water. Soon, he had stopped walking. He was running. "Archelaus" kept running through his mind.

Pray one Our Father and one Hail Mary and meditate on Joseph's story.

What do you do when the impossible becomes possible—when the improbable becomes real? Joseph had placed all his trust in God's will and God's word, the secret and elusive whisperings of a dream. That fundamental faith and trust had guided him into a marriage, into fatherhood, into Egypt—and now, was it really calling him back to Israel? Back to a place haunted by hatred and death?

The great puzzle of Joseph's life is that he accepted so much that most of us would otherwise refuse. He believed what most men wouldn't and believed the unbelievable. A pregnant virgin? An escape to Egypt? And now, a journey back to where it all began?

When I look back on my life, I spent most of my adulthood working for one company, in one place, with all the affirmation and security—paid vacations, regular raises, a pension—that went with it. I worked around the same people, in the same building, surrounded by familiar faces and voices and deadlines. A more adventurous person might call my life routine and predictable; I would call it comfortably secure—and it helped me support my wife and the life we built together.

During the early years of his life as a husband and father, Joseph had none of that. Honestly, I wonder sometimes how a man in those circumstances ever even had the opportunity to dream; for most of us, that would have meant sleepless nights and a lot of tossing and turning. But not so for Joseph. Something in his heart and soul spoke to him and said: "Trust in this. Believe. Do not be afraid. God has a plan. Go where he takes you."

How we need to learn from that! We need to remember the example of Joseph, whose quiet obedience and faith led him on the incredible journey of his lifetime—a lifetime of unknowing and mystery; a lifetime of loss and discovery; a lifetime, really, of miracles. He knew the miracle of realizing again and again God's vigilant love. He experienced the miracle of seeing salvation history unfold before his eyes and the miracle of knowing God's protection and learning, repeatedly, that a greater power was controlling his fate.

Do we have the sort of trust that Joseph had? Can we even imagine the kind of trust that would free us to see God acting in our world? Can we even begin to realize how much of our lives are, like Joseph's, miracles?

As they rolled up the blankets and packed a small basket of food, Mary looked at her husband's face and marveled. His usually furrowed brow was smooth. He didn't seem worried. He wasn't frightened. He had the same quiet intensity of the man she saw so often working over a piece of wood: focused, methodical, and absorbed in his thoughts.

"You're sure?" she asked him. "Not Bethlehem?"

He looked up at her and smiled.

"Yes. Nazareth. It was all so clear. We will go back to Nazareth. Galilee. Archelaus will not trouble us there. He won't even know." He took a deep breath. "We will be safe." He nodded toward

his son. "He will be safe." He took Mary's hand. "Trust me," he said. "Trust God."

She kept an eye on Jesus, playing with a ball of twine on the floor. Mary sighed. "It will be good," she began. "Good to be back with family. People we know."

He nodded. "We've spent so much time going from place to place," he said. "Maybe this is where God wants us to be for good." He stopped folding and packing and reached out to touch her cheek, reassuringly soft under his calloused palm. "Maybe we will finally be where we belong."

That evening, as the sun set and the air cooled, they set out, bound for Nazareth. They knew the way. The quiet of the night was broken only by the sound of small hooves hitting the earth. As they left the village—Mary again on the donkey, Jesus sitting astride in front of her, her arms holding him tightly—the stars began to appear, bright pinpricks in a black sky. Joseph looked up. Memories came flooding back. This was right. He just knew it. He couldn't hold back a smile. In a few days, they would be home.

In so many ways, the adventure of Joseph's life was about seeking to create a home. As a husband, as a father, as a faithful Jew, he traveled—often under difficult and dangerous circumstances—to find a place of shelter for his family, a home where they would be safe and comfortable.

From Nazareth, to Bethlehem, to Egypt, then back to Nazareth, his journey was sometimes desperate, sometimes uncertain. But it was always undertaken with a sense of holy trust and a desire to find a place to call home. It is easy to see why he is seen as a protector and guide for families in flight.

But he is also a patron for all of us trying to find sanctuary in a world that often doesn't offer it. When we feel lost, uneasy, afraid, there is St. Joseph: the one who undertook what were at best ill-advised journeys in the eyes of his contemporaries, and yet he made every place he stopped a home. More than that, he managed to make those places a home for Mary, the Mother of God, and the child Jesus.

It is worth remembering that home for so many of us can have mixed meanings. For some of us, it is a place of welcome and security; but for others, home is a place of harshness and hardship; and for still others, a place of hostility and violence.

For too many, home is a place that turns people out, not one that lets them in.

And for others, the very idea of home is something they dream about and yearn for. The place they call home may be a shelter, a street corner, a cardboard box. In some ways, these members of our human family may be closest to the Holy Family, who were forced to spend restless and anxious years without a real home. The Savior of the world, after all, came into that world in a time and place that had no room for him.

As we pray for those who have no place to call home, we might ask ourselves: Does God have a home in our lives? Our prayer should be that we strive to make room for him—earnestly, faithfully, selflessly. Every home can be like the one St. Joseph created—a home where Jesus and Mary find sanctuary and offer company, where God is made welcome.

REFLECT

How do I define home in my own life?

What does Joseph's profound trust in God teach me?

How can I strive to be as courageous as Joseph?

What are some ways I can open my home and my life more to God who is present there?

PRAY

> Traveling Joseph,
> when your family needed a home,
> you went where God sent you,
> seeking what was best for those you loved.
> No journey was too hard,
> no obstacle too great,
> no challenge too daunting,
> and you made every journey with courage and strength.
> How often I face the journeys of life with fear and worry!
> How I look for other, easier paths!
> Teach me to turn to you for help and for hope.
>
> Fatherly Joseph,
> walk with me when I feel afraid,
> and remind me how your love, fortitude, and faith
> guided your Holy Family safely home.
> Reassure me when I have doubts,
> and give my life's journey direction.
>
> Protective Joseph,
> be my companion when I feel lonely,

my friend when I feel abandoned,
my strength when I feel vulnerable in the storms of life.
Keep me close to you, as you stayed close to Mary and
Jesus,
so that you can help me find my way home.
Amen.

7.

JOSEPH SEARCHES FOR THE LOST JESUS

A Dreamer's Nightmare

Each year his parents went to Jerusalem for the feast of Passover, and when he was twelve years old, they went up according to festival custom. After they had completed its days, as they were returning, the boy Jesus remained behind in Jerusalem, but his parents did not know it. Thinking that he was in the caravan, they journeyed for a day and looked for him among their relatives and acquaintances, but not finding him, they returned to Jerusalem to look for him. After three days they found him in the temple, sitting in the midst of the teachers, listening to them and asking them questions, and all who heard him were astounded at his understanding and his answers. When his parents saw him, they were astonished, and his mother said to him, "Son, why have you done this to us? Your father and I have been looking for you with great anxiety." And he said to them, "Why were you looking for me? Did you not know that I must be in my Father's house?" But they did not understand what he said to them. He went down with them and came to Nazareth, and was obedient to them; and his mother kept all these things in her heart. And Jesus advanced [in] wisdom and age and favor before God and man.

Luke 2:41–52

WALK WITH JOSEPH

"How can this be?" Mary's eyes were pleading, desperate, then frightened. Her voice was choked with worry.

Joseph struggled for an explanation. "He, he . . . he always traveled with the other children," Joseph said. He closed his eyes, seeing Jesus again. He was sure he had seen him with his cousins. He could see it so clearly. His small head of dark hair, his plain brown robes. Joseph had told him, "Stay close. We will see you at supper." And Jesus had nodded. That was hours ago.

When the caravan had stopped on the way back to Nazareth, Joseph and Mary looked frantically. They spoke with every person they could find. No one had seen Jesus; they just assumed he was with his parents. After a long hour, the families collected themselves and prepared to go on.

"No," Mary said to her husband. "We have to find him. We need to go back to Jerusalem."

Joseph nodded, his cheeks burning. He blamed himself. Why hadn't he been more protective? Why hadn't he insisted that Jesus travel with them? Why had this happened?

They took their donkey and their belongings and told the other families they needed to look for their boy. He would be worried, they said. He might be frightened. He would surely be hungry. He loved to pray in the Temple, and they were certain he must have been near there. They had to go look for him. Some relatives wanted to join them, to help. A couple of the men insisted they go. But Joseph—battling feelings of desperation and shame—wouldn't hear of it. "It will be easier with just the two of us," he said, though he didn't entirely believe it. "We'll be fine." And he didn't entirely believe that, either.

"Pray for us," Mary told the cousins. "Pray for Jesus."

And then Joseph helped her up onto the donkey and they headed back down the rocky road they had already traveled. Joseph glanced over his shoulder and saw the caravan getting smaller and smaller, the noise of the animals and the carts and the people becoming fainter. The sun was getting closer to the horizon. They would probably be back at Jerusalem before dark.

As they walked in silence, Joseph's heart was heavy. His head ached. His body felt weak. How had this happened? What would they do when they got to Jerusalem? Where would they even begin? He could only imagine what Mary was thinking.

He looked up at her. Her eyes were closed. In the middle of all the fear and worry Joseph was experiencing, he was amazed at how calm she seemed. She looked tranquil, almost asleep. But her lips were moving. And Joseph heard the ancient words of the psalm, a prayer of pleading and hope.

"You are my God; be gracious to me, Lord;
to you I call all the day . . .
to you, Lord, I lift up my soul.
Lord, you are good and forgiving . . .
LORD, hear my prayer . . ." (Ps 86: 2–6).

Pray one Our Father and one Hail Mary and meditate on Joseph's story.

When I was working at CBS News, many of the true crime stories we produced for news magazine shows dealt with children in trouble—kidnappings, assaults, disappearances. They were urgent and upsetting—but sadly, after a while, they became almost cliché. I lost count of how many times I worked on an intro to a story and the producer suggested, "This is every parent's nightmare."

Thinking about Joseph and Mary's journey back to Jerusalem to search for their missing child, that phrase came back to me again. How would any parent feel if they discovered their child was missing? Had he run away? Was he abducted? Was he even still alive? How would they find him? At a certain point, the story goes from being a search to being a rescue. And nobody wants to even imagine the worst.

I think it was that way for the parents of Jesus. Joseph, the dreamer, must have felt as if he was living a nightmare. After all the years of trusting in God's mercy and guidance, he may have felt at this moment as though God had abandoned him. But surely the Lord would not abandon Jesus. Surely he would shield Mary from this kind of heartache and worry. Right?

When we consider what Mary and Joseph went through during those anxious days of searching for their son, we realize anew that no one escapes the very human reality of suffering, hardship, worry, and fear. Even the parents of God's only Son knew what it was like to lose someone they loved—and they knew the very real fear that he might have been lost for good.

Of all the sorrows Joseph knew in his life, this must have been one of the most upsetting. His son was vulnerable, alone, completely separated from those he trusted and the parents who cared for him. After all they had been through—all the journeys they had undertaken, trusting completely in God's will—was this how it was all going to end?

But as much as we think about what Jesus's parents went through, we also need to give prayerful consideration to what Jesus himself was going through.

Was he frightened? Worried? Did he feel abandoned and alone? Or, like Joseph, did he simply trust in God's guiding hand?

This episode should help us realize just how much Jesus shared our humanity—and how he, too, confronted his own helplessness. What did he do when he felt utterly alone and unsure of where to go or what to do? He found his way to the place where he would know true peace and hope. He turned to the One who would bring him consolation and joy.

———

Joseph and Mary started at the beginning. Once they had entered Jerusalem's gates, they went methodically from vendor to vendor, shopkeeper to shopkeeper. They looked for children his age—but to Joseph, every child looked too much like his own. They searched alleys and streets. They asked themselves, "Where would a twelve-year-old boy go?" They spoke with soldiers and butchers, rabbis and scribes.

Finally, they found themselves at a side door of the Temple and recognized one of the elders and stopped him as he was locking up for the night. They explained what had happened.

He managed a smile and grabbed Joseph's shoulder. "You finally came back!" he said. He cracked open the door, gestured. "He's in there. I couldn't believe it. But see for yourself."

Mary ran into the Temple. The crowd was thinning, but she spotted a small gathering of men in a far-off corner. Some were standing. A few were sitting. As she moved closer, she stopped. Joseph came up behind her and they were stunned. Jesus was in the middle of the group, a scroll open before him. He was speaking, gesturing, pointing to pieces of text. His eyes darted from face to face, as if addressing each listener individually.

And then he saw them. And he stopped, his face breaking into a wide smile. "Mother," he said softly. He put down the scroll and ran into her arms and hugged her tightly and then felt Joseph's hard hands gripping his shoulders and felt his father tremble. Joseph was fighting back tears but couldn't contain himself. He wept.

Joseph wiped the tears from his face, blinked, then smiled. Of course, he thought. Of course, this is where he would be. He raised his eyes, still damp with tears, and looked to the ceiling of the Temple and to someone far beyond that he could only imagine.

"Thank you," he whispered. "Thank you."

So what happened next? I wish we knew; but this is the last time we see St. Joseph in the gospels. He is never mentioned again—not by Mary, or Jesus, or anyone who might have known him or known about him. Like the boy Jesus visiting Jerusalem, Joseph is inexplicably lost.

But he can still be found. The tradition surrounding him continues his story.

One tradition holds that he died in old age, with Mary and Jesus by his side, after a lifetime of journeying, trusting, believing, and praying. He experienced "a happy death," entering eternal life in peace. As a result, Catholics frequently turn to Joseph as the patron of a "happy death," seeking his solace and companionship near the end of life.

You will often see depictions of him in his workshop—statues, paintings, and stained glass windows will show him with the boy Jesus, dutifully working with wood. What you rarely see, though, are depictions of Joseph with Jesus as a grown man (unless it's Joseph on his deathbed.)

But I like to think that Joseph can also be found in the most important work he undertook during his life: We see him in the man that Jesus became. From Joseph, Jesus would have learned the patience and diligence of being a carpenter. He probably learned from Joseph how to pray. An observant Jew, he regularly went with his family to the synagogue and, as scripture notes, to the Temple in Jerusalem.

We can speculate on what else his hidden years in Nazareth contained. Perhaps Jesus learned from Joseph how to look after his mother. He may have helped care for Joseph in his old age. Perhaps he kept the carpenter shop going and found a way to support his mother after Joseph died. Jesus would have lived the bulk of his life as the member of a large extended family, and no doubt become accustomed to rituals, traditions, and the routines of village life.

Joseph—his earthly father and role model—would forever be a part of Jesus's story, his experience, his memory. Jesus would have heard the stories of his birth, the flight to Egypt, the return to Nazareth. He would have known all that Joseph did for him and for his mother.

Undoubtedly, Jesus saw firsthand the sorrows and joys of Joseph and came to understand more fully the sorrows and joys of our world. The Incarnation was not just about God becoming human and dwelling among us; it was also about a boy growing into adulthood and experiencing all the struggles, setbacks, detours, and difficulties of living in a broken world.

Through life in that family, Jesus saw the human experience in all its wonder, heartache, and beauty. He saw the commitment and love of a husband and wife, a father and mother, and learned about the powerful bonds of family and history.

And in meditating on the sorrows and joys of Joseph, we gain new insight into our own—and find a spirit of resilience and tireless hope.

REFLECT

How have I responded when I felt helpless or hopeless?

What have I done when realizing I was lost?

Learning from St. Joseph, what can I do differently when I face unexpected setbacks?

What do Joseph's sorrows and joys teach me about my own life?

PRAY

Anxious Joseph,
you knew the sorrow, uncertainty, and dread
of any parent searching for a missing child.
Your love and concern for Jesus was so great,
this journey must have been heartbreaking.

Courageous Joseph,
you gave Mary strength and support.
During the days apart from Jesus,
you were the model of a consoling husband and loving
father.

Generous Joseph,
be with me during the most difficult times of my life.
Give me strength in moments of fear,
hope in times of despair,
and endurance in times of weakness,
so that I may continue with what God wants me to do.
Grant me the patience and fortitude
to always search for Christ in everyone and everything,
so that I may know the joy of discovering him
as he shows me the way to the Father, as he showed you.
Amen.

APPENDIX A

Additional Prayers to St. Joseph

Devotions to St. Joseph have endured throughout the centuries. He is beloved as a patron and intercessor for many circumstances and causes—for workers, parents, even people seeking a place to live. Announcing the Year of St. Joseph in 2020, Pope Francis wrote, "After Mary, the Mother of God, no saint is mentioned more frequently in the papal magisterium than Joseph, her spouse. My predecessors reflected on the message contained in the limited information handed down by the gospels in order to appreciate more fully his central role in the history of salvation. Blessed Pius IX declared him 'Patron of the Catholic Church,' Venerable Pius XII proposed him as 'Patron of Workers,' and Saint John Paul II as 'Guardian of the Redeemer.' Saint Joseph is universally invoked as the 'patron of a happy death.'"[4]

I've included here a number of prayers to the saint from a variety of sources. For many of them, the authorship is unknown or lost to history; they have been prayed for generations and brought inspiration and comfort to countless people who have used them to help befriend Joseph on the journey through life. In that spirit of intercessory hope, may these prayers help to draw all of us closer to the one who carried the young Jesus in his arms so that we, too, might feel the comfort of his strength, gentleness, and protection in our times of need.

TO YOU, O BLESSED JOSEPH

In his 1889 encyclical, *Quamquam Pluries* (On Devotion to St. Joseph),[5] Pope Leo asked that this prayer be added to the end of the Rosary especially during October, the month of the Holy Rosary. This prayer carries a partial indulgence.

> To you, O blessed Joseph, do we come in our afflictions,
> and having implored the help of your most holy Spouse,
> we confidently invoke your patronage also.
> Through that charity which bound you
> to the Immaculate Virgin Mother of God
> and through the paternal love
> with which you embraced the Child Jesus,
> we humbly beg you graciously to regard the inheritance
> which Jesus Christ has purchased by his Blood,
> and with your power and strength to aid us in our
> necessities.
>
> O most watchful guardian of the Holy Family,
> defend the chosen children of Jesus Christ;
> O most loving father,
> ward off from us every contagion of error and corrupting
> influence;
> O our most mighty protector,
> be kind to us and from heaven assist us
> in our struggle with the power of darkness.

As once you rescued the Child Jesus from deadly peril,
so now protect God's Holy Church
from the snares of the enemy and from all adversity;
shield, too, each one of us by your constant protection,
so that, supported by your example and your aid,
we may be able to live piously, to die in holiness,
and to obtain eternal happiness in heaven.
Amen.

HAIL, GUARDIAN OF THE REDEEMER!

Pope Francis[6]

> Hail, Guardian of the Redeemer,
> spouse of the Blessed Virgin Mary!
> To you God entrusted his only Son;
> in you Mary placed her trust;
> with you Christ became man.
> Blessed Joseph, to us too, show yourself a father
> and guide us in the path of life.
> Obtain for us grace, mercy, and courage,
> and defend us from every evil.
> Amen.

PRAYER BEFORE WORK TO ST. JOSEPH THE WORKER

Pope St. Pius X

O glorious St. Joseph,
model of all those who are devoted to labor,
obtain for me the grace to work in a spirit of penance
for the expiation of my many sins;
to work conscientiously,
putting the call of duty above my natural inclinations;
to work with thankfulness and joy,
considering it an honor to employ and develop by means of labor
the gifts received from God;
to work with order, peace, moderation, and patience,
never shrinking from weariness and trials;
to work above all with purity of intention
and detachment from self,
keeping unceasingly before my eyes death
and the account that I must give of time lost,
talents unused, good omitted, and vain complacency in success,
so fatal to the work of God.

All for Jesus, all through Mary,
all after thy example, O Patriarch, St. Joseph.
Such shall be my watchword in life and in death.
Amen.

DAILY NOVENA PRAYER TO ST. JOSEPH

Traditional

Pray once each day for nine consecutive days

O St. Joseph,
whose protection is so great, so strong,
so prompt before the throne of God,
I place in you all my interests and desires.
O St. Joseph,
do assist me by your powerful intercession
and obtain for me from your divine Son
all spiritual blessings through Jesus Christ, Our Lord,
so that having experienced here below your heavenly
power,
I may offer my thanksgiving and homage
to the most loving of fathers.
O St. Joseph,
I never weary of contemplating you with Jesus asleep in
your arms.
I dare not approach while he reposes near your heart.
Hold him close in my name and kiss his fine head from
me,
and ask him to return the kiss when I draw my dying
breath.
St. Joseph, patron of departing souls, pray for me.
Amen.

ACT OF CONSECRATION TO ST. JOSEPH

Traditional

O dearest St. Joseph,
I consecrate myself to your honor and give myself to you,
that you may always be my father, my protector,
and my guide in the way of salvation.
Obtain for me a great purity of heart
and a fervent love of the interior life.
After your example, may I do all my actions for the greater glory of God,
in union with the Divine Heart of Jesus and the Immaculate Heart of Mary!
And do, O Blessed St. Joseph,
pray for me that I may share in the peace and joy of your holy death.
Amen.

PARENTS' PRAYER TO ST. JOSEPH

Traditional

O glorious St. Joseph,
to you God committed the care of his only begotten Son
amid the many dangers of this world.
We come to you and ask you to take under your special
protection
the children God has given us.
Through holy Baptism they became children of God
and members of his holy Church.
We consecrate them to you today,
that through this consecration they may become your
foster children.
Guard them, guide their steps in life,
form their hearts after the hearts of Jesus and Mary.

St. Joseph, who felt the tribulation and worry of a parent
when the child Jesus was lost,
protect our dear children for time and eternity.
May you be their father and counselor.
Let them, like Jesus, grow in age as well as in wisdom and
grace
before God and men.
Preserve them from the corruption of this world
and give us the grace one day
to be united with them in heaven forever.
Amen.

PRAYER FOR A HAPPY DEATH

Traditional

> O Blessed Joseph,
> you gave your last breath in the loving embrace of Jesus
> and Mary.
> When the seal of death shall close my life,
> come with Jesus and Mary to aid me.
> Obtain for me this solace for that hour—
> to die with their holy arms around me.
> Jesus, Mary, and Joseph, I commend my soul,
> living and dying, into your sacred arms.
> Amen.

MEMORARE TO ST. JOSEPH

Traditional

Remember, O most pure spouse of the Virgin Mary,
my beloved patron,
that never it has been heard
that anyone invoked your patronage
and sought your aid without being comforted.
Inspired by this confidence I come to you
and fervently commend myself to you.
Despise not my petition,
O dearest foster father of our Redeemer,
but accept it graciously.
Amen.

PRAYER TO KNOW ONE'S VOCATION

Catholic Doors Ministry, Humboldt, Canada[7]

O Great Saint Joseph,
you were completely obedient to the guidance of the Holy
Spirit.
Obtain for me the grace to know the state of life that God,
in his providence, has chosen for me.
Since my happiness on earth,
and perhaps even my final happiness in heaven,
depends on this choice, let me not be deceived in making
it.
Obtain for me the light to know God's Will,
to carry it out faithfully,
and to choose the vocation which will lead me to eternal
happiness.
Amen.

PRAYER TO ST. JOSEPH, PATRON OF THE UNIVERSAL CHURCH

Traditional

O most powerful patriarch, Saint Joseph,
patron of that universal Church
which has always invoked thee in anxieties and
tribulations;
from the lofty seat of thy glory
lovingly regard the Catholic world.
Let it move thy paternal heart to see the mystical spouse of
Christ
and his vicar weakened by sorrow
and persecuted by powerful enemies.
We beseech thee, by the most bitter suffering thou didst
experience on earth,
to wipe away in mercy the tears of the revered pontiff,
to defend and liberate him,
and to intercede with the Giver of peace and charity,
that every hostile power being overcome and every error
being destroyed,
the whole Church may serve the God of all blessings in
perfect liberty.
Amen.

PRAYER TO ST. JOSEPH TO SELL A HOUSE

A popular custom (to some a superstition) holds that if you bury a small statue of St. Joseph upside down on your front lawn and say this prayer every day, your home will sell more quickly. The origins of this odd custom are a mystery. Some contend it was started by an order of nuns in the Middle Ages, who buried holy medals of the saint when they needed help building a convent; others say it's a practice begun by German carpenters, who buried statues of St. Joseph in the foundations of new homes. The idea became more widespread, evidently, in the late twentieth century, when it became easy and cheap to market plastic statues to anxious homeowners.

> O St. Joseph,
> you who taught our Lord the carpenter's trade,
> and saw to it that he was always properly housed,
> hear my earnest plea.
> I want you to help me now as you helped your foster child Jesus,
> and as you have helped many others in the matter of housing.
> I wish to sell this [house/property] quickly, easily, and profitably
> and I implore you to grant my wish by bringing me a good buyer,
> one who is eager, compliant, and honest,
> and by letting nothing impede the rapid conclusion of the sale.

Dear St. Joseph,
I know you would do this for me
out of the goodness of your heart and in your own good
time,
but my need is very great now
and so I must make you hurry on my behalf.

St. Joseph,
I am going to place you in a difficult position
with your head in darkness
and you will suffer as our Lord suffered,
until this [house/apartment/property] is sold.
Then, St. Joseph, I swear before the cross and God
Almighty,
that I will redeem you and you will receive my gratitude
and a place of honor in my home.
Amen.

PRAYER FOR A HAPPY DEATH

Traditional

Glorious St. Joseph,
foster father and protector of Jesus Christ!
To you do I raise my heart and hands
to implore your powerful intercession.
Please obtain for me from the kind Heart of Jesus
the help and graces necessary for my spiritual and
temporal welfare.
I ask particularly for the grace of a happy death,
and the special favor I now implore (insert intention).

Guardian of the Word Incarnate,
I feel animated with confidence that your prayers on my
behalf
will be graciously heard before the throne of God.

O glorious St. Joseph,
through the love you bear to Jesus Christ,
and for the glory of his name,
hear my prayers and obtain my petitions.
Amen.

PRAYER TO FIND A JOB

Traditional

Dear St. Joseph,
you yourself once faced the responsibility
of providing the necessities of life for Jesus and Mary.
Look down with fatherly compassion upon me in my
anxiety
with my present inability to support my family.
Please help me find gainful employment very soon,
so that this great burden of concern will be lifted from my
heart
and that I am soon able to provide for those whom God
has entrusted to my care.
Help me guard against discouragement,
so that I may emerge from this trial spiritually enriched
and with even greater blessings from God.
Amen.

PRAYER IN TIMES OF ANGUISH AND DIFFICULTY

Pope Francis Announcing the Year of St. Joseph

"Every day, for over forty years, following Lauds I have recited a prayer to Saint Joseph taken from a nineteenth-century French prayer book of the Congregation of the Sisters of Jesus and Mary. It expresses devotion and trust, and even poses a certain challenge to Saint Joseph."[8]

> Glorious Patriarch Saint Joseph,
> whose power makes the impossible possible,
> come to my aid in these times of anguish and difficulty.
> Take under your protection
> the serious and troubling situations that I commend to you,
> that they may have a happy outcome.
>
> My beloved father, all my trust is in you.
> Let it not be said that I invoked you in vain,
> and since you can do everything with Jesus and Mary,
> show me that your goodness is as great as your power.
> Amen.

APPENDIX B

Praying the Seven Sorrows Devotion as a Group

LEADER:

Let us pray.
All make the Sign of the Cross.
Good and gracious God:
In reflecting on St. Joseph's sorrows and joys,
may we see how he shared the same hardships and hopes
we all have,
and may we feel his closeness, his companionship, and his
protecting love.
May he help us grow ever closer to you
and to your Son—the one Joseph loved as his own—
Jesus Christ.

ALL:

Amen.

JOSEPH'S FIRST SORROW

Joseph Decides to Divorce Mary, but Then an Angel Brings Good News

READER:

A reading from the holy Gospel According to St. Matthew.

Now this is how the birth of Jesus Christ came about. When his mother Mary was betrothed to Joseph, but before they lived together, she was found with child through the holy Spirit. Joseph her husband, since he was a righteous man, yet unwilling to expose her to shame, decided to divorce her quietly. Such was his intention when, behold, the angel of the Lord appeared to him in a dream and said, "Joseph, son of David, do not be afraid to take Mary your wife into your home. For it is through the holy Spirit that this child has been conceived in her. She will bear a son and you are to name him Jesus, because he will save his people from their sins." All this took place to fulfill what the Lord had said through the prophet:

"Behold, the virgin shall be with child and
   bear a son,
and they shall name him Emmanuel,"

which means "God is with us." When Joseph awoke, he did as the angel of the Lord had commanded

him and took his wife into his home. He had no
relations with her until she bore a son, and he
named him Jesus. (Mt 1:18–25)

LEADER:

We begin our journey with Joseph,
remembering the sorrow that pierced his heart,
when he planned to leave Mary to avoid a scandal.
But we remember, too, the joy that uplifted his heart:
the words of an angel
that foretold humanity's salvation.
May we always keep our hearts open
to God's work in our lives,
leading us, like Joseph, to trust more deeply in his love.

Let us pray.

ALL:

Holy Joseph,
you lived the simple and predictable life of a carpenter,
planning and building, dreaming and praying.
Yet, you saw God take the clean lines and sharp angles of
an ordinary life
and bend them with his perfect hand.

Righteous Joseph,
God chose you, just as he chose Mary,
to help bring his Son into the world.
Through the mysterious beauty of a dream,
you said yes to God's will,

yes to accepting a role unrivaled in human history,
yes to being the guardian of God's most precious treasure,
and the father of humanity's hope.

Trusting Joseph,
when we receive news we never wanted to hear,
help us to be open to God's will.
Comfort us in our fear, console us in our anxiety,
and remind us in this fallen world of God's never-failing
grace.
Help us every day to live as you lived,
with trust in God that ultimately brings true joy.
We ask this through the source of your joy,
the one you loved as your own son,
Jesus Christ.
Amen.

All pray together an Our Father, Hail Mary, and Glory Be.

JOSEPH'S SECOND SORROW

Joseph Sees Jesus Born in Poverty
but Then Sees Him Celebrated by the Heavenly Hosts

READER:

A reading from the holy Gospel according to St Luke.

And Joseph too went up from Galilee from the town of Nazareth to Judea, to the city of David that is called Bethlehem, because he was of the house and family of David, to be enrolled with Mary, his betrothed, who was with child. While they were there, the time came for her to have her child, and she gave birth to her firstborn son. She wrapped him in swaddling clothes and laid him in a manger, because there was no room for them in the inn.

Now there were shepherds in that region living in the fields and keeping the night watch over their flock. The angel of the Lord appeared to them and the glory of the Lord shone around them, and they were struck with great fear. The angel said to them, "Do not be afraid; for behold, I proclaim to you good news of great joy that will be for all the people. For today in the city of David a savior has been born for you who is Messiah and Lord. And this will be a sign for you: you will find an infant wrapped in swaddling clothes and lying in a manger." And suddenly there was a multitude of the heavenly host with the angel, praising God and saying:

"Glory to God in the highest
and on earth peace to those on whom his
   favor rests." (Lk 2:4–14)

LEADER:

Joseph watched in sorrow
as his son was born into poverty,
entering a world that had no room for him.
But Joseph's sorrow turned to joy
when he heard angels singing the praises of his newborn
son
and saw kings bow before him.
May we find reassurance in Joseph's quiet faith.
May we seek to find God's glory all around us,
even in the most humble, fragile, and small.

Let us pray.

ALL:

Searching Joseph,
you journeyed far to seek shelter and security in Bethlehem,
only to find instead a place that had no room
for the Savior of the world.
We can only imagine the disappointment and heartbreak
you felt watching the Son of God come into the world
as a pauper—with no true home,
and little shelter from the elements and the hardships of life.

Anxious Joseph,
the sorrow you felt is the sorrow of every parent
dreaming of a good life for their children

and often wishing things could be better than they are.
But your steadfastness and faith remind us:
Trust always in God's tender mercy!
Give thanks to him in all circumstances,
believe in his plan, pray for his guidance,
ask for his consolation and strength.

Hopeful Joseph,
help us to gaze toward God in the darkest of nights,
and see the stars.
Teach us how to count our blessings,
numbering God's miracles in our own lives,
with humility and steadiness and faith.
May we always see in your example
a model of quiet confidence:
an example of fidelity and strength.
We ask this in the name of your son, Jesus,
who came into an unwelcoming world
to bring all of us a sense of welcome,
possibility, and hope.
Amen.

All pray together an Our Father, Hail Mary, and Glory Be.

JOSEPH'S THIRD SORROW

Joseph Suffers at His Son's Circumcision, Then Rejoices in the Name of Jesus

READER:

> A reading from the holy Gospel according to St. Luke.
>
>> When eight days were completed for his circumcision, he was named Jesus, the name given him by the angel before he was conceived in the womb. (Lk 2:21)

LEADER:

Is there anything more painful for a parent
than the suffering of an innocent child?
With a sorrowful heart, Joseph watched as Jesus was circumcised
and the baby cried out in pain.
But Joseph soon knew the inexpressible joy
of hearing his newborn son receive the name
that was first pronounced by the angel: Jesus.
Amid the sufferings of our own lives,
may the loving name of Jesus offer us consolation and hope.

Let us pray.

ALL:

Compassionate Joseph,
you loved the Son of God as if he were your own flesh and blood,
suffering with him and sharing every pain of his young life,
shedding tears of sorrow at his circumcision when he cried out.

Comforting Joseph,
you cradled the baby Jesus with a father's love,
wiping away every tear,
with tenderness and strength,
using the strong calloused hands of a carpenter
to console and caress and calm.

Giving Joseph,
you gave such care to the Son of God,
as you heard the cries that foretold the suffering of Calvary
and the redemption of our world.
Hear our prayers this day.
Be our inspiration, our consolation, and our guide.
Help our hearts to be more caring,
guide our hands to be more gentle,
and whenever we feel the pains and pangs of life,
remind us that we are not alone,
but that you are by our side,
just as you were with your son, Jesus.
Amen.

All pray together an Our Father, Hail Mary, and Glory Be.

JOSEPH'S FOURTH SORROW

Joseph Hears a Prediction of Mary's Suffering,
and Then Hears of the Glory of the World's Redemption
through Jesus

READER:

A reading from the holy Gospel according to St.
Luke.

When the days were completed for their purification according to the law of Moses, they took him up to Jerusalem to present him to the Lord, just as it is written in the law of the Lord, "Every male that opens the womb shall be consecrated to the Lord," and to offer the sacrifice of "a pair of turtledoves or two young pigeons," in accordance with the dictate in the law of the Lord.

Now there was a man in Jerusalem whose name was Simeon. This man was righteous and devout, awaiting the consolation of Israel, and the holy Spirit was upon him. It had been revealed to him by the holy Spirit that he should not see death before he had seen the Messiah of the Lord. He came in the Spirit into the temple; and when the parents brought in the child Jesus to perform the custom of the law in regard to him, he took him into his arms and blessed God, saying:

> "Now, Master, you may let your servant go
>   in peace, according to your word,
> for my eyes have seen your salvation,

> which you prepared in sight of all the peoples,
> a light for revelation to the Gentiles
> and glory for your people Israel."

The child's father and mother were amazed at what was said about him; and Simeon blessed them and said to Mary his mother, "Behold, this child is destined for the fall and rise of many in Israel, and to be a sign that will be contradicted (and you yourself a sword will pierce) so that the thoughts of many hearts may be revealed." (Lk 2:22–35)

LEADER:

Traveling to the Temple in Jerusalem,
Joseph heard a painful prophecy for Mary.
But he also heard another prophecy:
that the child Jesus would bring glory to Israel.
Once again, he faced the sorrow of human suffering
and then the joy of immeasurable hope.
May Joseph's quiet compassion
bring us closer to all who suffer,
and may God's grace bring healing to all.

Let us pray.

ALL:

Listening Joseph,
you went to the Temple in Jerusalem out of obedience and devotion,
with a generous heart,
full of love for God and for your family.

You heard a prophecy you never expected,
words of salvation and glory—but also of sorrow and pain.

Suffering Joseph,
we can only imagine the anguish and sorrow you felt
on hearing the words of the holy and aged Simeon—
how you worried for the family you loved,
and how you wondered what God had in store.

Strong Joseph,
help us to live with a sense of surrender and trust,
giving back to God some of what he has given to us.
Teach us to accept any challenge, bear any burden,
and walk any difficult path with the same love, courage,
and sense of purpose as you did.
Help us to stay focused on God's will,
so that we may face the future without undue fear
and with joy everlasting.
Amen.

All pray together an Our Father, Hail Mary, and Glory Be.

JOSEPH'S FIFTH SORROW

Joseph and His Family Flee to Egypt, Where Idols Fall before Jesus

READER:

> A reading from the holy Gospel according to St. Matthew.
>
> The angel of the Lord appeared to Joseph in a dream and said, "Rise, take the child and his mother, flee to Egypt, and stay there until I tell you. Herod is going to search for the child to destroy him." Joseph rose and took the child and his mother by night and departed for Egypt. He stayed there until the death of Herod, that what the Lord had said through the prophet might be fulfilled, "Out of Egypt I called my son." (Mt 2:13–15)

LEADER:

In a time of terror,
Joseph fled with his family to Egypt,
to save the life of his newborn son.
He experienced the sorrow and anxiety of a refugee,
going to an unknown land to start a new life.
But he also came to know the joy of a new world,
one that was transformed because of Jesus.
We pray for all who are journeying like Joseph—
struggling for a better life for those they love,
trusting always that God will guide them
where they were meant to be.

Let us pray.

ALL:

Courageous Joseph,
you answered the words of an angel
by setting out toward a foreign land,
going into the desert of a world you did not know
to save the child you loved,
the child who himself was born to save the world.
Help us in moments of weakness and doubt,
in times of uncertainty and fear,
to find the courage to live with faith,
trusting God to guide our way.

Devoted Joseph,
be our companion, our guide in the deserts of life.
When we feel lost, give us direction;
when we despair, give us hope;
when we feel sorrow, offer us the joy of your friendship.

Sheltering Joseph,
you found a home for Jesus and Mary when they sought refuge.
Lead us where we need to go
when we flee the dangers and difficulties of life.
As once you protected the family you loved,
be our protector and our shelter,
so that we may find peace.
May your family be forever our family,
and may they always hold us in their loving embrace.
Amen.

All pray together an Our Father, Hail Mary, and Glory Be.

JOSEPH'S SIXTH SORROW

Joseph Fears Returning to Israel, Then Is Told in a Dream to Go to Galilee

READER:

A reading from the holy Gospel according to St. Matthew.

When Herod had died, behold, the angel of the Lord appeared in a dream to Joseph in Egypt and said, "Rise, take the child and his mother and go to the land of Israel, for those who sought the child's life are dead." He rose, took the child and his mother, and went to the land of Israel. But when he heard that Archelaus was ruling over Judea in place of his father Herod, he was afraid to go back there. And because he had been warned in a dream, he departed for the region of Galilee. He went and dwelt in a town called Nazareth, so that what had been spoken through the prophets might be fulfilled, "He shall be called a Nazorean." (Mt. 2:19–23)

LEADER:

What courage it took to leave Egypt
and return to the land of Herod and his son, Archelaus!
Led by a dream,
guided by an angel,
Joseph overcame his fears and his sorrow,
and bravely took his family where God led them.
Together, they knew the simple joy of life together in Nazareth.

May we always seek to go where God leads us
and trust in his direction for our lives.

Let us pray.

ALL:

Traveling Joseph,
when your family needed a home,
you went where God sent you,
seeking what was best for those you loved.
No journey was too hard, no obstacle too great,
no challenge too daunting,
and you made every journey with courage and strength.
How often we face the journeys of life with fear and worry!
How we look for other, easier paths!
Teach us to turn to you for help and for hope.

Fatherly Joseph,
walk with us when we feel afraid,
and remind us how your love, fortitude, and faith
guided your Holy Family safely home.
Reassure us when we have doubts,
and give our life's journey direction.

Protective Joseph,
be our companion when we feel lonely,
our friend when we feel abandoned,
our strength when we feel vulnerable to the storms of life.
Keep us close to you, as you stayed close to Mary and Jesus,
so that you can help us find our way home.
Amen.

All pray together an Our Father, Hail Mary, and Glory Be.

JOSEPH'S SEVENTH SORROW

Joseph Searches for the Child Jesus and Finds Him in the Temple

READER:

A reading from the holy Gospel according to St. Luke.

Each year his parents went to Jerusalem for the feast of Passover, and when he was twelve years old, they went up according to festival custom. After they had completed its days, as they were returning, the boy Jesus remained behind in Jerusalem, but his parents did not know it. Thinking that he was in the caravan, they journeyed for a day and looked for him among their relatives and acquaintances, but not finding him, they returned to Jerusalem to look for him.

After three days they found him in the temple, sitting in the midst of the teachers, listening to them and asking them questions, and all who heard him were astounded at his understanding and his answers. When his parents saw him, they were astonished, and his mother said to him, "Son, why have you done this to us? Your father and I have been looking for you with great anxiety." And he said to them, "Why were you looking for me? Did you not know that I must be in my Father's house?" But they did not understand what he said to them. He went down with them and came to Nazareth, and was obedient to them; and his mother kept all

these things in her heart. And Jesus advanced [in]
wisdom and age and favor before God and man.
(Lk 2:41–52)

LEADER:

This final journey of Joseph
was full of worry, sorrow, uncertainty, and helplessness—
Searching for his missing son.
But it was a journey that ended in joy
when Joseph found Jesus in the safety of God's house.
May Joseph help guide all of us who are searching—
and lead us to Jesus.

Let us pray.

ALL:

Anxious Joseph,
you knew the sorrow, uncertainty and dread
of any parent searching for a missing child.
Your love and concern for Jesus was so great,
this journey must have been heartbreaking.
Courageous Joseph,
you gave Mary strength and support.
During the days apart from Jesus,
you were the model of a consoling husband and loving
father.

Generous Joseph,
be with us during the most difficult times of life.
Give us strength in moments of fear,
hope in times of despair,

and endurance in times of weakness,
so that we may continue what God wants us to do.

Grant us the patience and fortitude
to always search for Christ in everyone and everything,
so that we may know the joy of discovering him
as he shows us the way to the Father, as he showed you.
Amen.

All pray together an Our Father, Hail Mary, and Glory Be.

LEADER:

Almighty God,
You have given us Joseph as a model of
quiet strength, obedience, and trust.
May we learn from his sorrows and joys
how to trust always in your mercy and goodness,
and with Joseph's example of faith, hope, and love,
draw closer to your Son, Jesus Christ.
Amen.

NOTES

1. Pope Francis, "*Patris Corde*: Apostolic Letter of the Holy Father on the 150th Anniversary of the Proclamation of St. Joseph as Patron of the Universal Church," December 8, 2020, https://www.vatican.va/content/francesco/en/apost_letters/documents/papa-francesco-lettera-ap_20201208_patris corde.html.

2. Pope Benedict XVI, *Jesus of Nazareth: The Infancy Narratives*, trans. Philip J. Whitmore (New York: Image, 2020), 40.

3. William Barclay, *The Gospel of Luke* (Louisville, KY: Westminster John Knox Press: 1975, 2001), 29.

4. Francis, "*Patris Corde*."

5. Pope Leo XIII, "*Quamquam Pluries*," August 15, 1889, https://www.vatican.va/content/leo-xiii/en/encyclicals/documents/hf_l-xiii_enc_15081889_quamquam-pluries.html.

6. Francis, "*Patris Corde*."

7. https://www.catholicdoors.com/prayers/english/p00306 .html.

8. Francis, "*Patris Corde*."

Greg Kandra serves as a deacon in the Diocese of Brooklyn and is a senior writer at the Catholic Near East Welfare Association. He is the author of *A Deacon Prays* and writes *The Deacon's Bench* blog. Kandra was a writer and producer for CBS News from 1982 to 2008 for programs including *CBS Evening News with Katie Couric*, *Sunday Morning*, *60 Minutes II*, and *48 Hours*. He also served for four years as a writer and producer on the live finale of the hit reality show *Survivor*.

Kandra has received two Peabody Awards and two Emmy Awards, four Writers Guild of America Awards, three Catholic Press Association Awards, and a Christopher Award for his work. He also was named 2017 Clergy of the Year by the Catholic Guild of Our Lady of the Skies Chapel at JFK International Airport. He earned a bachelor's degree in English from the University of Maryland. Kandra cowrote the acclaimed CBS documentary *9/11*. He contributed to three books, including Dan Rather's *Deadlines and Datelines* and a homily series. His work has been published in *America*, *US Catholic*, *Busted Halo*, and *The Tablet*. He has been a regular guest on Catholic radio. Kandra is the author of four books.

Kandra lives with his wife, Siobhain, in the New York City area.

https://thedeaconsbench.com/
Facebook: @TheDeaconsBench
Twitter: @DeaconGregK

ALSO BY
DEACON GREG KANDRA

The Essential Prayer Book for Catholic Deacons

A Deacon Prays
Prayers and Devotions for Liturgy and Life

A Deacon Prays is a practical, daily companion that speaks to deacons as no other book has because it is written by a deacon for deacons. Deacon Greg Kandra shares prayers to help strengthen a deacon's spiritual life and richly enhance his ministry.

There are prayers

- for daily life and seasons;
- for service in particular ministries;
- to patron saints;
- of devotion tailored for deacons;
- of petition and intercession; and
- marking special times in the life of a deacon.

This is an indispensable addition to any deacon's prayer corner, briefcase, or glove compartment, and will be a popular gift for ordinations, birthdays, holidays, and other special occasions in the life of a Catholic deacon.

"A timeless treasury."
—Deacon Harold Burke-Sivers
Catholic radio host and author of *Father Augustus Tolton*